EKSTASY

EKSTASY:
Out-of-the-Body Experiences
—— DAVID BLACK ——

UNITY SCHOOL LIBRARY
UNITY VILLAGE, MISSOURI 64065

The Bobbs-Merrill Company, Inc.
Indianapolis/New York

The author wishes to thank Petra Cabot for permission to reprint "Antigonish" by Hughes Mearnes.

Copyright © 1975 by David Black

All rights reserved, including the right of reproduction in whole or in part in any form
Published by the Bobbs-Merrill Company, Inc.
Indianapolis   New York

ISBN 0-672-51972-0
Library of Congress catalog card number 74-17679
Designed by Ingrid Beckman
Manufactured in the United States of America

First printing

For Deborah

Acknowledgments

I would like to thank Phyllis Westberg for her encouragement, and Diane Giddis for her thorough and excellent editorial advice. I would also like to thank Stefanie Tashjian-Woodbridge for reading part of the book in manuscript and Blue Harary for the help he gave me in finding my way around the parapsychological subculture.

Table of Contents

I have a little shadow that goes in and out with me,
And what can be the use of him is more than I can
see.
He is very, very like me from the heels up to the
head;
And I see him jump before me, when I jump into
my bed.

The funniest thing about him is the way he likes to
grow—
Not at all like proper children, which is always very
slow;
For he sometimes shoots up taller like an
india-rubber ball,
And he sometimes gets so little that there's none of
him at all.

He hasn't got a notion of how children ought to
play,
And can only make a fool of me in every sort of
way.
He stays so close beside me, he's a coward you can
see;
I'd think shame to stick to nurse as that shadow
sticks to me!

One morning, very early, before the sun was up,
I rose and found the shining dew on every
    buttercup;
But my lazy little shadow, like an arrant sleepy-head,
Had stayed at home behind me and was fast asleep
    in bed.

Robert Louis Stevenson, "My Shadow"

My face was buried in the folds of her neck, her legs had started to clamp me, the ashtray toppled off the bed table, the universe followed—but at the same time, incomprehensibly and delightfully, I was standing naked in the middle of the room, one hand resting on the back of the chair where she had left her stockings and panties. The sensation of being in two places at once gave me an extraordinary kick; but this was nothing compared to later developments.

Vladimir Nabokov, *Despair*

As I was going up the stair
    I met a man who wasn't there!
He wasn't there again today!
    I wish, I *wish* he'd stay away!

Hughes Mearnes, "Antigonish"

PART 1

THE SHADOW'S SHADOW

In his mind, Findlayson had already escaped from the boat, and was circling high in the air to find a rest for the sole of his foot. His body— he was really sorry for its gross helplessness— lay in the stern, the water rushing about its knees.

"How very ridiculous!" he said to himself. . . . "The poor beast is going to be drowned. . . . I'm on shore already. Why doesn't it come along?"

RUDYARD KIPLING, *"The Bridge Builders"*

CHAPTER 1

Introduction

BOB HALL THREW HIMSELF from the small Cessna airplane and counted. He tumbled through space, like Alice dropping down the rabbit hole. As he waited for his automatic parachute to open, he watched the Coolidge, Arizona, airport falling up into the sky. Twisting around to check his lines, he found his main and emergency parachutes tangled; and, as though he were understanding something that had been puzzling him for a long time, he realized he was plunging 3400 feet to the desert below.

On that Sunday afternoon in October, 1972, Bob Hall was convinced he was dead. He didn't think, *When I hit the runway, I'm dead.* He felt, as he kept falling, that he was dead already and that his soul had left his body, that his consciousness had separated from his flesh.

He was aware of how hot the sun was, of the particu-

lar blue of the sky, of the plane circling overhead and
the shadow of the plane on the desert, at the same time
that he was experiencing—watching dispassionately
from above and yet vividly reliving—every other important moment of his past. His nineteen years collapsed into a multiple, simultaneous flashback. Four
years old, playing with friends on the lawn outside his
parents' house; skiing; going to military school; strad-
dling a motorcycle; arriving on his first day at Arizona
State University. . . . Tens of thousands of scenes, all
real; tastes, smells, sounds, all real; the feel of getting
bucked off a horse, the touch of snow spraying his face,
the pressure of the parachute harness, real. And then
he saw his body dropping at sixty miles per hour, a dark
wriggling shape against the vast uprushing brown of
the desert.

Rob Winkle, Bob Hall's Pi Kappa Psi brother and
friend, had jumped before Bob; and, when he described what happened, his voice was religiously sub-
dued, as though awe and terror had created a magic
circle in his memory and he crossed that boundary hesitantly.

"I looked up, saw Bob's chute start to open, and
looked away. Below, I saw the van some friends were
in moving across the desert. When I was about three
hundred feet above ground, I heard a loud noise. I
looked up and saw Bob fifty or a hundred yards away,
falling. I saw his face. It was terrifying. He was yelling,
'Help! Help! Someone help me!' I didn't realize what
was happening. I saw him hit, crumple up, and go over
onto his right side. His chute came over him like a
shroud. I thought, *He's dead.* Then, he sat up."

"The whole thing lasted about forty-five seconds,"
Hall said. "I don't remember the impact. The first thing

I remember after landing was getting up. The first thing I said to the person who came over to me was, 'I dreamed it all.' You know how when you're talking to somebody and you forget what you're saying, and all of a sudden it comes back into your memory as though you've said it before, but maybe you haven't really said it before? Well, that's how I felt when I got up.

"I landed feet down. The impact was so hard, I snapped the top part of my body, and my nose hit my belly. Try to touch your nose to your belly. That's how hard I hit. My nose hit a little metal box the size of two cigarette packs, an automatic opening device that sets a little above waist level. The fall pulverized my nose, knocked out my front teeth, and cut my lip, but that's all that happened.

"The whole thing was amazing, especially the feeling when I was falling that my soul had gone out of my body and I was looking down at myself. Just as an overseer, an observer that wasn't there."

During the two months after I heard about how Bob Hall had slipped from his body while dropping through space, I began stumbling upon other accounts of out-of-the-body experiences, odd descriptions that at first pleased me because they could not be explained, and then disturbed me for the same reason.

If I mentioned Hall's accident at a party, friends or acquaintances responded, not to the 3400-foot fall (parachutists often survive extraordinary falls) or to the curious life-review Hall reported, but to his account of how his consciousness had temporarily left his body; and they would tell me their own out-of-the-body episodes, the facts usually blurred by their embarrassment at having indulged, even unwillingly, in the occult, which like some exotic sexual practice both fascinates and repels the great-great-grandchildren of the Enlightenment by promising (as sex does) an essential violation of privacy. If consciousness can leave the body as easily as water spilling over the rim of an overfilled glass, then what happens to the hard edge of individuality? And what nightmares of demonic possession such speculation can trick into being!

I don't think I would have clipped the news item about Hall's accident or subsequently sought out Hall to verify the story if he had only been describing some out-of-the-body flight (which I would have dismissed as the tic of a religious imagination). But, although it was not necessarily related to his out-of-the-body experience, the fact he had survived such an incredible fall was real; that snagged my attention.

An old friend, Janice Carduner, who had grown up within a mile of my childhood home in Springfield, Massachusetts, was one of the people responsible for convincing me that out-of-the-body episodes were common enough and—in their effect on those who experienced them—real enough to justify investigation. She told me she often had the sensation of being outside of her body.

"The most recent experience," Janice said, "happened just a few weeks ago. I was standing in the kitchen, bringing the dishes to Stuart [her husband], who was washing them. I started to think, *I'm married to a person who wears glasses.* And, as soon as I thought that, I suddenly felt myself out of my body. I was behind and slightly to the left of my physical body, and I could see the physical me which was standing in between the two windows in the kitchen, looking at Stuart. I was very scared because I couldn't control it. My consciousness stayed out of my body until I went outside the house. It was almost like the other me grabbed the physical me by the arm and escorted me out."

"I didn't notice anything strange," said Stuart. "She just suddenly got very quiet."

Although Janice seemed a Hollywood model for a modern witch—a narrow triangular face that made her look, when happy, like a Burne-Jones goddess and, when angry, like a praying mantis—she had no interest in the occult; and she did nothing to cultivate her out-of-the-body episodes.

"Every time I used to describe having this kind of experience to someone," she said, "the experience would happen again."

"Is it happening now?" I asked her.

"No," she said, "but I have the feeling it could happen—it's hard to describe—like the sensation you get with *déjà vu,* but not the memory part, only the mental discomfort."

Mental discomfort. Janice's description sprung traps in my imagination. The summer had been heavy with tales of psychics, astrologers, apocalypse; I had never heard so many people discussing the unknown with such knowledgeable conviction. There had been an energy shortage—cars couldn't get enough gasoline and the electricity output of generator plants all over the country had been cut back enough to slow records and tapes, so that voices and music seemed slightly flat. A discomforting sound, as threatening to the stability of our culture as the rumble of revolutionists' guns from beyond the next hill. It was as though, if our fossil fuels were failing us, people were determined to discover some more dependable energy, psychic energy.

Another childhood friend, Doug Fauntleroy, whom I

had not seen since 1969 when he joined the Black Panther Party and severed relations with all whites, visited me a few weeks after Janice had told me her story. Prompted by my casual mention of Bob Hall's fall, he described an experience he'd had.

"I think it was November, 1965," Doug said. "I had taken six months off from Shimer College to earn some money so I could finish school, and I was working the three-to-eleven shift at a Chrysler body-stamping plant, where I was spot-welding floorpans, doors, fenders—assembly-line work. It was the height of the auto production season, so we had to work overtime. Nine hours a day, eight hours on Saturday. I was always exhausted.

"I used to hitchhike back and forth to work ten or fifteen miles, part of it along Nine Mile Road, a very long flat wide street going into Detroit. The night I'm thinking of, it had just stopped raining. Pitch black. No moon, just stars. There were open fields beside the road for quite a few blocks, although if you looked across the fields you could see shopping centers.

"Every three or four blocks was a traffic light, and the lights were timed, synchronized with each other so they were all green or all red for about thirty seconds. But they were fixed so you couldn't go but so fast down the road.

"I was bored, waiting for a ride, so I started trying to figure out how many lights I could hold in my mind's eye at the same time, focusing on all of them so none of them were blurry and so, when they were all one color, I could actually see that one color all the way down the street.

"As I was doing that, I noticed that there were reflections of the lights in all the puddles too, and I was having difficulty distinguishing which was the puddle and which was the light. I began to separate them by being very still and very quiet, not allowing my mind to have any thoughts—which was a very strange feeling. It got to the point where I was extremely still; and at that point, I don't remember exactly what happened, but I had the sense that I could be out of my body.

"I was no longer aware of the traffic lights, even though I was still looking down the street. It was very windy, and I remember the sound of the telephone wires kind of buzzing in the wind overhead. Suddenly, I had this feeling that I was eighty or ninety feet up in the air looking down at my body. I felt as though I were still inside my head, but I was up in the air and I could look down and see my body below me, shivering in my coat."

Although I became curious about these out-of-the-body tales, I at first resisted their lure. I have a noon-time temperament; I prefer my world sunny and shadowless. And out-of-the-body experiences traditionally belong to a dim world inhabited by faddists, widows with mothball-smelling sweaters and bulging bankbooks, and astral travelers—a subculture which is just beginning to shed most of the zany mumbo jumbo that for the past hundred years has kept parapsychological research out of the scientific Big Top and in the Side Show.

But this ghostly self that slips through history and literature as elusively as it slid through Bob Hall's flesh when he was plummeting through the Arizona sky continued to haunt me. Doug—like Janice—was sure that the sensation of being outside his body had been real, but he was not convinced that his consciousness had actually separated from his physical self. He wavered: it must have; it couldn't have. The conflict between rationalism and mysticism in society was being played out in separate battles in individuals; and I began wondering how many small victories mysticism must have before the culture would subtly shift away from the traditional Western view of reality. I wondered, in fact, if the shift had already occurred.

I began questioning people directly about the out-of-the-body experience. It seemed as good a test as any. At random gatherings about thirty per cent of those I'd ask would say yes, that's funny, they did once have an experience like that. . . .

Tom Blackwell, a painter who lived in New Hampshire an hour's drive from the small Massachusetts village where I was living, stopped by on his way to New York the same week I had talked with Doug; and, aware of my growing fascination with the out-of-the-body phenomenon, he told his story:

"I'd rented a little house outside of Yokohama when I was in the Navy stationed in Japan. I was nineteen. I'd never had any experience with drugs. I brought a girl to this place one time. We were making love in this room. All of a sudden, my consciousness left my body, and I was above myself, looking down at this scene of us making love. I could literally see myself."

He paused and smiled, stumped by how to express the feeling of identifying with a body and a mind that were no longer joined.

"I mean," he said, "something saw me making love with this girl. Or I—wherever I was—saw something with her on the bed."

Tom's confusion was the play of a psychic argument as ancient as the first humanoid that felt the itch of self-consciousness as it coupled with its mate. What part of man was animal appetite? What part was something more? Were humans closer to the angels or to the beasts?

A week later I stopped to talk to Dick French, a young carpenter I'd recently met who worked at a farm not far from where I lived. As he showed me around his shop, we talked of various local matters. Then I told him the story about Bob Hall, and of the other out-of-the-body experiences I'd been running across.

"I know what that's like," he said. "When I'm really physically tired, I'll be lying in bed, and I'll feel this surge of energy coming up my back, over my head, stopping sort of behind my eyes. And I'll be paralyzed. Except if I try to move my arm, for instance, like this"—he swept his arm in toward his chest as though he were gesturing for someone to come closer—"it'll feel like my arm moved. It'll feel absolutely real. But my physical arm will still be paralyzed at my side. Once I tried to get up, and I had the feeling of floating out of my body up toward the ceiling. It's uncomfortable, but I never thought much about it before."

A few weeks later, when I met his girlfriend, Emily Samuels, she said, "I can't tell when Dick has that feeling, because he just gets very still. Although sometimes he gets rigid like this." She stiffened, her arms at her sides as though she were standing at attention. "He tries to communicate that it's happening by moving an eyebrow or some small sign like that."

Little by little, I surrendered to my curiosity, although trying to pin down this strange double was like wrestling with a shadow. It may be real, but how can you get hold of it? I began jotting down case histories and keeping random notes of anything which seemed relevant.

Melissa Stevenson, a young woman I met shortly

after I'd begun my tentative research, told me about the experience she'd had during her sophomore year at Skidmore College, in Saratoga Springs, New York, when she dreamed she was standing in front of her bureau fiddling with her contact lenses.

"It was very realistic," she said. "I knew I was dreaming in my bed, but I also felt I was at the dresser. In the morning, Maureen, my roommate, told me she woke up in the middle of the night and saw me at the dresser putting in, or taking out, whichever it was, my contact lenses. Then she looked over and saw another me sleeping in my bed."

Melissa sat in a ladderback chair, her feet propped on the warm fender of the wood-burning stove in the servants' kitchen of a Dublin, New Hampshire, mansion where she and her husband were caretakers. On a stormy night the house would look like a C-movie mad doctor's castle in which an innocent journalist, poking about for a scoop, confronts a slimy horror; and in my search after this phantom phenomenon, I felt as naive and apprehensive as a hero in such a movie.

"I've had other dreams," Melissa said, "flying dreams, when I may have left my body. I'll look down at a road I'm flying over and see all the little landmarks, stones, the leaves, or the snow, and it will seem real. But I've never had another experience as weird as the one at Skidmore."

"We had a room in a dormitory," said Maureen Magee, Melissa's former roommate, who when I spoke to her was living in Naples, Florida. "My bed was on one side, with my dresser in front of the bed, and Melissa's was the same on the other side. This was six or seven years ago when we were nineteen or twenty. I woke up and saw Melissa standing in front of her bureau, leaning over, apparently taking out her contacts. Then I looked over at her bed and saw her sleeping there. I kept looking from one to the other, trying to figure out which one was Melissa. But I couldn't figure it out. Both looked normal."

She didn't walk over to check, she explained, because the experience had not seemed threatening and so it didn't matter; both were Melissa, and Melissa was safe. Although she seemed slightly embarrassed discussing the episode, Maureen described the extraordinary event so nonchalantly that I began to suspect that somehow Melissa's bilocation had not violated the physical laws of either Melissa's or Maureen's world; both accepted the paranormal as normal.

People who had no interest in the occult seemed to have no trouble including the occult in their worlds. Stuart and Janice Carduner, Doug Fauntleroy, Tom Blackwell, Dick French and Emily Samuels, Melissa Stevenson and Maureen Magee, all the people I discussed out-of-the-body experiences with seemed uneasy talking about the subject, but comfortable with the fact that it existed. Their toleration of the extraordinary bothered me as much as the descriptions of the events themselves. Listening to them I was as unnerved as when, ten years old, I walked on the bridge that passed through the inside of the glass world globe in the *Christian Science Monitor* building in Boston. What had upset me then was not only the sense of having my world reversed, seeing the planet inside out, but also the realization that if I fell, I would shatter the glass continents below me. Embarking on an investigation of something I didn't believe in and didn't want to believe in left me with the same queasy feeling that if I took a wrong step I might end by accidentally smashing up my familiar world.

But by the end of the summer, I'd become obsessed

with this strange doubling of the self. Even the identical twins in the subway advertisement for Doublemint gum had begun to look vaguely occult. I capitulated and started seriously to reconnoiter this odd corner of the psychic underworld, hoping that somehow investigating this particular phenomenon would give me a method of exploring my own ambivalent feelings about psychic phenomena in general.

Most psychologists have no trouble admitting that there is an authentic *subjective* experience in which the perceiving "I" is temporarily organized from a point of view outside the physical body; but recently, as a result of post-psychedelic curiosity about altered states of awareness, a new generation of researchers has begun accommodating itself to the uncomfortable notion that the out-of-the-body experience may be exactly what our senses tell us it is—an occasion when the conscious mind takes a vacation from the cage of the flesh.

Dr. Robert Morris at the Parapsychological Research Foundation in Durham, North Carolina; Dr. John Palmer at the University of Virginia; Celia Green at the Institute of Psychophysical Research in Oxford, England; Dr. Karlis Osis at the American Society for Psychical Research; Dr. John Lilly, who pioneered communication experiments with the bottle-nosed dolphin; Dr. Stanley Krippner at the Maimonides Medical Center in Brooklyn, New York; Dr. Harold Puthoff and Mr. Russell Targ at the Stanford Research Institute; Dr. Charles T. Tart from the University of California at Davis; and Edgar D. Mitchell, the Apollo-14 astronaut, have all puzzled over the phenomenon. Although each of them wades through parapsychological speculation with the caution of a pessimist who is convinced he is about to slip on some slick, unexplainable fact and sink, they have all suggested—some more hesitantly than others—that the out-of-the-body experience is to some indeterminate degree objectively real.

Objectively real, however, is a phrase loose enough to tangle up many conflicting opinions; and interpretations explaining the nature of this objective reality vary so much that the out-of-the-body experience becomes a voluminous valise of a concept, capable of holding just about any idea you might want to toss in.

Theosophists, for the past half-century the most responsive audience to out-of-the-body stories, see the phenomenon as conclusive evidence that there exists a vehicle of the soul. Theosophical tracts are crowded with drawings of dots close together, demonstrating the solidity of physical flesh, and dots spaced farther apart, revealing the flimsiness of the etheric body— proof as convincing as the television aspirin commercial showing an animated cartoon of the Bs getting from the stomach to the headache faster than the ineffective As.

The religious find in out-of-the-body experiences clues to sainthood. The diaspora of the sixties psychedelic revivalism seizes on out-of-the-body experiences as manifestations of a utopian psychic evolution. Psychiatrists, as though words have a magical ability to tame weird, wild experiences, usually dismiss any out-of-the-body experience as being simply *autoscopy,* the projection of a consciousness unable to accept responsibility for a particular act, a narcissistic hallucination that denies the power of death. They conscientiously neglect any evidence of extrasensory perception that may have occurred during the incident. Otto Rank, one of Freud's early associates, described autoscopic episodes as products of autoerotic longings. Carl Gustav Jung, who experienced out-of-the-body flights, more generously explained them as moments when you dive into the pool of the collective unconscious, leaving your ego like a forgotten bathing suit on shore. Physicists studying the phenomenon join hands with the Theosophists and define the experience in terms of vibrational levels and imperceptible, perhaps imaginary subatomic particles.

These explanations for out-of-the-body episodes, the scientific as well as the fantastic, are myths—they adequately describe the phenomena without necessarily being true—and each researcher descends into his private unknown to charm up from the depths those concepts which can rationalize the public unknown. The theories mirror the researchers' obsessions. The materialistic find only science; the religious find only God.

But, if the search for this slippery double is in some part mythical, the myth is not Orpheus wandering through the underworld among disembodied spirits, but Theseus in the labyrinth stalking his half-human prey: a fabulous hunt for the self which casually steps from the body, leaving the mind ajar.

CHAPTER 2

The Eternal Mimic

FOR THE FIRST FEW MONTHS of my search through the occult underworld, the most basic question—What is an out-of-the-body experience?—seemed impossible to answer. I might as well have been asking: "What is the shape of thunder?" or "How large is a laugh?" Attempting to characterize the phenomenon in detail was as difficult as trying to pick up a drop of water with thumb and forefinger. For most of the people whose stories I collected, the experiences were either ineffable or casually mystifying, and the accounts were different enough from each other to resist easy generalizations.

Bob Hall's consciousness left his body completely, organizing itself at a point which seemed to be outside the accepted structure of space and time. Janice Carduner's consciousness left her body completely but remained a fixed point in our familiar four-dimensional world. Melissa Stevenson's consciousness split—bilocated—inhabiting for a moment both her physical body and a non- or partially physical body.

The various accounts of out-of-the-body experiences shared only the feelings that consciousness (the part of the self which is the perceiving "I") had separated from the physical body and that, during the out-of-the-body state, the separated consciousness functioned as an ego —the criteria which any authentic out-of-the-body experience must fulfill.

The out-of-the-body experience, then, is different from the experience of transcendence, when the ego, losing its identity, dissolves into the All, and different from the exercise of extrasensory perception, when consciousness remains within the body and one perceives events at a distance from many, or no, points of view.

Futhermore, the out-of-the-body experience does not appear to be a case of telepathy (extrasensory contact between two minds) or clairvoyance (extrasensory contact between a mind and either an event or an object), because neither telepathy nor clairvoyance presupposes a subjective sensation that consciousness has separated from the physical body. Telepathy and clairvoyance, although not the out-of-the-body experience itself, may be operating with out-of-the-body sensations. Or out-of-the-body perception may be an entirely distinct phenomenon. Much of contemporary out-of-the-body research is, in fact, focused on this problem. Part of the difficulty may be semantic, but it is likely that the confusion in labeling the out-of-the-body experience reflects a substantial difference between that phenomenon and either telepathy or clairvoyance.

Every double is not necessarily an out-of-the-body self, although there is a reductionist tendency among many occultists and parapsychologists to shuffle together related experiences in an effort to develop a unified theory for all paranormal phenomena which would, by its comprehensive simplicity, demand belief. Reincarnating souls, ghosts, projections of the double, and phantoms of the living such as *vardøgers* and *doppelgängers*, have all been nudged forward as examples of out-of-the-body experiences.

The essence that in many traditions quits the physical shell when the body dies may not be the same as the soul that slips from the flesh when the body is alive, even though in some cultures both are identified by the same name. The quick have no way of knowing; the dead have no way of telling. And near-death incidents do not give us any clue as to whether or not the out-of-the-body self and the soul are identical, because, while the incidents may be useful windows onto the out-of-the-body experience, they are not necessarily dry-runs for death. Near-death sensations may not predict what you feel when you actually die, any more than foreplay adequately mimics the rush of orgasm.

This hesitancy to delve into the moment-after-the-last-moment prohibits the use of certain interesting documents such as the *Bardol thödol (Tibetan Book of the Dead)*—a Fielding's guide to the hereafter that describes the paths through the newly dead, unenlightened soul's self-created heavens and hells back to rebirth—which could be plundered, and often are, for what seem to be references to the out-of-the-body experience. The protocol for dying and being reborn reflects many of the same assumptions behind a belief in a soul that can leave the living body. Yet the central concern of the *Tibetan Book of the Dead* is not with a consciousness that temporarily leaves and returns to the same body, but with a soul that transmigrates, borrowing a new life without losing its essential identity. And, because there is no proof for reincarnation, after-death events must lie outside the study of out-of-the-body experiences, until some certified Lazarus returns with the scoop.

For the same reason that the experience of a soul after death can't be considered proper material for a study of out-of-the-body experiences, any apparition of the dead seen by the living (all ghosts whether the sheeted variety, wisps, mists, or Topper's ectoplasmic chums) must fall outside the scope of the investigation. They may be manifestations of the ultimate out-of-the-body experience; but again, since there is no reliable evidence for life-after-death—voices from the grave too often are more than modulated by mediums—the inquiry into out-of-the-body experiences must stop at the grave's edge.

Phantoms of the living, like the Norwegian *vardøger*, a double that appears at a place shortly before the flesh-and-blood body arrives, and the *doppelgänger*, a ghostly double that haunts its material counterpart may seem to be the products of out-of-the-body experiences. However, in these phenomena consciousness remains within the physical body rather than inhabiting the double—a distinction as fine as the tuning that eliminates the ghost from a fuzzy television image, but an important one nonetheless. *Vardøgers* and *doppelgängers*, according to tradition, usually have no consciousness. Since an out-of-the-body experience is an episode when consciousness leaves the body, *vardøgers* and *doppelgängers*, though possibly related to out-of-the-body doubles, and respectable phantoms in their own right, cannot be included in an examination of out-of-the-body phenomena.

The Scottish *tàslach,* a "forerunner" like the *vardøger* which will walk up the path, open and close the cottage door, and hang up a ghostly cap minutes or sometimes hours before its flesh-and-blood original arrives, and the Scottish *tamhasg,* a specter of the living that, like the *doppelgänger,* leads an existence independent of the physical body, also fall outside the range of an investigation into out-of-the-body experiences. As John Gregorson Campbell wrote in *Witchcraft and Second Sight in the Highlands of Scotland:*

> The whole doctrine of these apparitions of the living, or, as they are called in Cumberland, *swarths,* and premonitions of coming events, proceeds on the supposition that people have an *alter ego,* which goes about unknown to themselves, with their voices, features, form, and dress, even to their shoes, and is visible to those who have the unhappy gift of second sight. . . . This phantasm, or other self, is not the life or the spirit of the person it represents. He has nothing to do with it . . . and in general the *taibhs* [a broad Gaelic term for phantoms, including all kinds of specters of the living] is independent of all thought, or action, or emotion of the person it represents.

Some doubles, difficult to classify, skulk like shades in limbo on the edge of a study of out-of-the-body experiences. During an out-of-the-body episode, for example, you may not realize your consciousness has left your flesh; and, seeing the physical body, you may assume it was a specter—a loophole large enough to shove a few *doppelgängers* through.

Among the Siryanians, a Finnish people of Eastern Russia, the *ort,* originally a soul-double that could separate from the body, has shed its traditional identity and is now considered to be a guardian angel rather than the visible form of a consciousness that has temporarily left the flesh.

And the Slavic *Mora*, which is, according to myth, a man or a woman who leaves the body at night and travels around the countryside sucking the blood of sleeping neighbors, sounds more like a vampire than an out-of-the-body adept.

The projection of the double is, like the *vardøger*, a ghostly twin of the flesh-and-blood man which has no consciousness of its own; but, unlike the *vardøger*, it is the product of a conscious attempt to project the image of the self across a distance.

In April, 1909, the psychologist William James, one of the founders of the American Society for Psychical Research, published an account of a Harvard University colleague's projection of the double in *The Journal of the American Society for Psychical Research* (Vol. II, No. 4).

> My dear Dr. James [the professor wrote]: . . . the thing occurred in the latter part of 1883 or the first part of 1884. At this time A and I were seeing each other very frequently, and we were interested, among other things, in that book by Sinett on Esoteric Buddhism. . . .
>
> One evening, about 9:45 o'clock, or, perhaps, nearer 10 . . . I resolved to try whether I could project . . . to the presence of A. . . . I opened my window, which looked toward A's house . . . and sat down in a chair and tried as hard as I could to wish myself into the presence of A. . . . I sat there in that state of wishing for about ten minutes. Nothing abnormal in the way of feeling happened to me.
>
> Next day I met A, who said something to this effect . . .

"Last night about ten o'clock I was in the dining room at supper with B. Suddenly I thought I saw you looking in thru the crack of the door at the end of the room . . . I got up and looked . . . but there was nobody there."

Although the projection is actively and willfully accomplished and although something of the self may separate from the body, consciousness remains within the flesh-and-blood frame. "Nothing abnormal in the way of feeling" happens to the projector. The projection, like a slide image flashed on a wall, cannot perceive or act independently. Although, as James said, this "type of phenomenon is so rare and, if not to be explained by accidental coincidence, so important, that all reported cases of it should be recorded," it is not an out-of-the-body experience.

Certain cases of bilocation, where there is no hard evidence that consciousness has either completely or partially left the physical body, are also not necessarily out-of-the-body episodes—as, for example, in the story told about St. Francis Xavier, who, while enroute from Japan to China in 1552, was seen during a storm sharing a small boat with fifteen frightened sailors who had abandoned ship at the same time he was on board the mother ship, assuring the sailors who had not panicked that their absent companions were safe. Or as in the story of St. Anthony of Padua who, on Holy Thursday of 1226, knelt in the Church of St. Pierre du Queyrrix at Limoges, France, pulled his cowl over his head, and, according to popular legend, at that moment also appeared at the other end of town where he took part in a service with another congregation which had been waiting for him. Or as in that of St. Alphonse de' Liguori, who blacked out after celebrating the mass on September 21, 1774, and revived twenty-four hours later, explaining, "I have been assisting the Pope [Clement XIV], who has just died"—a claim made all the more bizarre by the fact that it was alleged that Liguori had been seen at the dying pontiff's bedside.

In each of these three cases legend has conspired with time to cloud whatever truth lies behind the tales, and none of the people involved specifically described having the sensation that consciousness had left the body. The stories about Francis Xavier and Anthony of Padua are reported from the point of view of someone watching the action; we have no serious accounts of what the two saints themselves felt. Although Alphonse de' Liguori claimed to "have been assisting the Pope," his statement could possibly be ascribed, not to an out-of-the-body episode, but to clairvoyance. All three cases, if they are authentic, may certainly be closely related to the out-of-the-body phenomenon, but none of them can be safely presented as clear-cut examples of out-of-the-body functioning.

"Lucid" dreams—dreams in which the sleeper is aware he is dreaming—although possibly related to out-of-the-body experiences, are not accompanied by the sensation that consciousness has actually separated from the body. Any adventures the dream-self undergoes seem to occur in an inner landscape, not in a reality external to the sleeper.

Some psychiatrists have opened the door onto the bleak possibility that an out-of-the-body experience may be the expression of a gentle schizophrenia. Reversing that suggestion, a few out-of-the-body researchers have hinted that some schizophrenics may be the victims of out-of-the-body jaunts, not madness. But, according to Dr. N. Lukianowicz in "Autoscopic Phenomena," published in the *A.M.A. Archives of Neurology and Psychiatry* (Vol. 80, No. 2, August, 1958), the experience of seeing yourself is "an extremely rare occurrence" in schizophrenia and "is equally rare in the next most frequent psychological disorder, the group of *depressions*"—observations which check the complementary dismissals that this common experience is merely craziness or that craziness is merely being out of your body, not out of your mind.

CHAPTER 3

OOBEs In Myth
And History

THE OUT-OF-THE-BODY EXPERIENCE, like Saint-Réal's idea of the novel, is a mirror moving down a road, reflecting the landscape it passes through, a contentless experience which is given shape by the prejudices and superstitions of the society in which it occurs.

The ancient Chinese were adept at exteriorizing the soul while the body was alive; and, according to legend, the Emperor Shun, the first man to learn how to send his soul on a magical flight, learned the skill from two women, Nü Ying and O Huang, daughters of the previous Emperor Yao (who, like Shun, was rumored to have double pupils in his eyes). Shun was described as "flying like a bird" during his out-of-the-body episodes, but the description is a familiar shorthand for a complex event: "The legendary history and folklore of China abound in examples of 'magical flight,'" wrote Mircea Eliade in

Shamanism, "and . . . even in the ancient period well-informed Chinese regarded 'flight' as a plastic formula for ecstasy." The ecstatic, like the Emperor Shun, was a "type of magician . . . whose art consisted primarily in 'exteriorizing' his soul, in other words, 'journeying in spirit.' "

In India, arhats (Buddhist saints), kings, and magicians often claimed to have the power of out-of-the-body flight, a gift certain twentieth century Indian holy men, like Sai Baba, reportedly possess.

In ancient Egypt, as in many other cultures, the self that separated from the living body was distinguished from another soul which stayed with the body after death and often suffered a second death of its own—a subtlety borrowed by contemporary Theosophists to explain cases of trilocation, when consciousness perceives from a third point in space both a physical body and a ghost-image of the physical body.

The Japanese believe that in *Mugen no Kyo* (one of four traditional trance states, which also include ecstasy, *Muchu;* coma, *Shisshi, Konsui-Jotai;* and hypnotic stupor, *Saimin-Jotai*) the soul travels from the body. The Great-Land-Master, *Oh-kuni-nushi* (who was the quasi-historical successor to the Japanese storm-god), once saw his "rough soul"—which with a "mild soul" formed the complete soul, *tama-shii,* in Shinto mythology—moving toward him from the sea.

The out-of-the-body self materializes among the Karens of Burma as the *kelah* or *la,* which—though not the soul—causes death if it strays too long from the body; among the Melanesians as *atai,* a disembodied spirit self; and among the Wild River Shoshone of Wyoming as *navujieip* (one of three souls) which, if you are a powerful medicine man, can leave the living body to wander both on earth and in the spirit world. The spooky Self appears among the Iroquois as a semi-corporeal double, identical in all its parts to the physical body. It turns up in Africa among tribes at the southern end of Lake Nyasa as the *mzimu*, the soul that can speak and act like a man, and among the Ba-huana, a Bantu tribe, as *doshi*, a double that sometimes appears in dreams.

The Hausa of Nigeria, the Dieri of Australia, the Solomon Islanders, the Fox Indians (an Algonquian tribe which, during the Black Hawk War in 1832, was driven from Illinois and Wisconsin), and the Dayaks of Borneo all believe that there is a soul-double which abandons the sleeping body to travel on its own. The Akawaio Caribs of British Guiana believe the spirit of a shaman on occasion can float from the flesh. The Mongol Buryats of Siberia believe that every shaman has a double, *sunäsun*, which can leave the body to wander about in a semimaterial form that can speak to and be seen by others. The Iglulik Eskimos claim that one's disembodied consciousness can sometimes see the body that it inhabited, stripped of flesh, as a skeleton—an odd experience reported by psychiatrists in some cases of autoscopy. In Australia, the Ngatatara believe that the *iruntarinia*, spirit doubles, perform in ritual ceremonies. And in New Zealand, the Maoris have reported that the *wairua*, shadowy doubles, are mistaken for the living bodies they duplicate.

In the Western World, perhaps the earliest mention of the out-of-the-body experience occurs in the legends of Abaris, who according to some accounts lived in

Greece about 770 B.C., and who was an adept of "magical flight," able, like the Emperor Shun, to journey in his spirit. And, according to Herodotus and Pliny, Aristeas of Proconnesus, a magician who lived eighty years later, could leave his body at will and was often seen in two places at the same time.

Pliny also reported the rumor that Epimenides of Crete, who lived in the sixth century B.C., could leave his body to travel in many lands, a trick he learned after emerging from a cave in which he had napped for fifty-seven years—thirty-seven years longer than Rip Van Winkle. In Washington Irving's tale Van Winkle woke to find that his grown son was "a precise counterpart" of himself, a discovery that suggests a dim reflection of the out-of-the-body experiences Epimenides indulged in after he had awakened.

Herotimos of Clazomenae, a philosopher of the Ionic School who probably lived in the sixth century B.C.—his dates are as obscure as the magic he practiced—possessed a soul which, according to Pliny's *Natural History*, "was in the habit of leaving his body, and wandering into distant countries, whence it brought back numerous accounts of various things, which could not have been obtained by any one but a person who was present. . . ."

Herotimos traveled extensively in the spirit until, according to Caesar de Vesme's *Peoples of Antiquity*, "his wife, profiting by one of his 'soul' excursions, once caused him to be regarded as dead, and to be cremated."

Clearchus of Soli, one of Aristotle's pupils, demonstrated to his teacher that the soul could leave and return to the body by tapping a sleeping boy with a wand which, he claimed, attracted the soul, drawing it out of the flesh. While the soul was gone, Clearchus slugged the boy a few times to prove that the body was inanimate; and when the soul returned, the boy reported on events that had occurred at a distance.

In the first century A.D., a California of the soul, when the mystery cults from the East invaded the Roman Empire, there is evidence that the out-of-the-body experience was one of the initiation rites of the Orphic mysteries. The novice ascended into heaven, which was both a physical climb up a ladder and, like the concept of magical flight in ancient China, "a plastic formula for ecstasy."

Around the beginning of the third century A.D., Tertullian observed that there was a "power we call ecstasy, in which the sensuous soul stands out of itself, in a way which even resembles madness."

But it wasn't until later in that century that Plotinus, the Egyptian philosopher who founded Neoplatonism and who once planned to create a republic in Southern Italy based on Plato's teachings, refined the concept of ecstasy (from the Greek: *ex*-out + *histanai* to cause to stand; that is, to stand outside). In the *Fourth Ennead,* Plotinus wrote: "Many times it has happened: Lifted out of the body into myself; becoming external to all other things and self-encentered; beholding a marvelous beauty. . . ." "Out of the body . . . and self-encentered" is a fair definition of the out-of-the-body experience: there still is a self for awareness to be centered within, although that self is no longer identified with the physical body. This ecstasy, however, was in Plotinus's philosophy only a way station on the route to transcendental union with the All.

First, consciousness separates from the physical and fixes itself in a particular point in space and time; and then consciousness releases the ego, like a rocket dropping its second stage as it roars out of earth orbit, and returns egoless to God.

Girolomo Cardano, a sixteenth century mathematician, physician, and astrologer, wrote:

> When I go into a trance I have near my heart a feeling as though the spirit detached itself from the body, and this separation extends to all the body, especially the head and neck. After that, I have no longer the idea of any sensation, except of feeling myself outside my body.

In the eighteenth century, John Gay, author of *The Beggar's Opera,* reported experiencing the sensation of having two consciousnesses, one which seemed to be associated with the physical body, the other which seemed independent of it. And Goethe, in his autobiography, described how once, while riding on horseback:

> I saw myself—not with my real eyes, but those of my mind—riding on horseback toward me on the same road and clothed in a garment such as I had never worn: its color was the gray of pike, with some gold in it. As soon as I roused myself from this dream, the figure had completely disappeared. It is strange, however, that after eight years I found myself on this same road . . . wearing the garment of which I had dreamed and which I was wearing not from choice, but from accident.

An out-of-the-body episode mixed with pre-cognition.

Alfred de Musset, George Sand, Guy de Maupassant, and August Strindberg all reported stumbling upon themselves. (According to Francis Steegmuller's biography, de Maupassant once complained, "Every other time I come home, I see my double. I open the door, and I see him sitting in my armchair.") However, only de Musset's account of abruptly and literally being beside himself sounds like an authentic out-of-the-body episode. The stories of Sand, de Maupassant, and Strindberg seem more like reflections of the modish obsession with the *doppelgänger* which seized Europe during the nineteenth century.

CHAPTER 4

New Mysteries For Old

BY THE END of the nineteenth century, an explosion of interest in hypnotism and hysteria had triggered a series of experiments in out-of-the-body phenomena. Students of animal magnetism mesmerized their subjects and then stuck pins in the air inches above the subject's flesh, trying to prove that the out-of-the-body body was an ethereal envelope surrounding the flesh—a strange experiment which would only make sense if one assumed the pin also had an ethereal envelope which acted upon the subject's ghostly body.

While magnetists like Charles Lancelin, Dr. H. Baraduc, Hector Durville, and Albert de Rochas were studying exteriorization of sensibility in France, in England Frederic William Henry Myers, one of the founders of the British Society for Psychical Research and the man who coined the term *telepathy*, was touching on the subject as part of his general survey of the quickly expanding field of psychical research. Myers distinguished between telepathy, projection of the double, and out-of-the-body experiences, which he described as bilocation ("The sensation of being in two different places at once . . .") and traveling clairvoyance ("The faculty or act of perceiving, as though visually, with some coincidental truth, some distant scene . . .").

Edmund Gurney, a friend of Myers, another of the founders of the British Society for Psychical Research, and co-author with Myers (and Frank Podmore) of *Phantasms of the Living*, also studied out-of-the-body experiences, as did Sir Oliver Lodge, a physicist who was a Fellow of the Royal Society and president of the British Society for Psychical Research.

Between 1912 and 1915 in Paris, Pierre Emile Cornillier hypnotized a young model named Reine and sent her consciousness sailing through space in experiments reminiscent of the demonstration of the soul's mobility which Clearchus of Soli performed for Aristotle. While Reine was in a trance, Cornillier gave her the addresses of various of his friends, asking her to visit them in her out-of-the-body state. She accurately described the contents of the unfamiliar apartments in these experiments—which could indicate either out-of-the-body functioning or clairvoyance coupled with the sensations that consciousness had separated from the physical body.

The phenomenon had possessed the popular imagination by the end of the First World War. In 1918 Jack London published *The Star Rover*, a novel based on the out-of-the-body flights experienced by his friend Ed Morrell during the five years Morrell had spent in solitary confinement in San Quentin prison. By the 1920s, partly as a result of the influence of Theosophy, the out-of-the-body experience had become wedded to the concept of astral travel, an occult notion that combines the sensation of consciousness separating from the physical self with a mythology involving vibrational levels, planes of existence, and astral bodies.

This theory of the astral body, which Theosophists believe to be the quasi-physical vehicle of the traveling soul, can be traced back to Proclus, a fifth century Neoplatonist who was an initiate into both the Orphic and Chaldaic mysteries, a vegetarian, and a magician who (according to legend) could bring rain and stop earthquakes. During the first half of the twentieth century the astral conceit flourished. Hugh Callaway (who masked himself for his audience as Oliver Fox), the French occultist Yram, Sylvan Muldoon and Hereward Carrington (the founder of the American Psychical Institute), and a whole squadron of astral fliers produced manuals which explained how to launch and navigate the astral body and which described the hallucinated creatures—demons and guardian angels, imps like those that used to perch on the shoulders of the good-little-bad-boy in the comics—that crowded their imaginations. The out-of-the-body experience was incorporated into a complex mythology which had only coincidentally to do with the singular sensation of consciousness leaving the flesh, a mythology which was a crazy quilt of Eastern religions, Neoplatonism, cabalistic tradition, and Christian mysticism.

By the early 1950s dozens of paperbacks, cannibalizing both F. W. H. Myers's serious studies of psychic phenomena and the occult books published by Callaway, Yram, Muldoon and Carrington, further confused out-of-the-body experiences with the mythology of astral travel. The same schizoid impulse in American society which nourished the double-identity comic book heroes (Captain Marvel, Superman, Batman, and all their imitators) manifested itself as a fascination with the concept of a spirit-double. We were all secretly Clark Kent-Superman, able to fly through the air and flick meteors from their paths—a reflection of how individually powerless and nationally powerful we felt and of how finely, as a result of that split, we were separating personal ethics from social morality.

All the contradictions in the culture, which in a decade would crack along this psychic fault under the pressure of the Vietnam War, found a safe expression in occult books like those on astral projection. We could be as materialistic as we wanted and still be spiritual; we did not have to resolve the two passions. Even the vocabulary of those books allowed the reader to look backward into a safe mythological past and forward into an uneasy but promising technological future at the same time by plucking words and phrases from physics and chemistry and redefining them as quasi-religious concepts. The fourth-dimension became a popular haunt for astral wanderers; Heisenberg's uncertainty principle (subatomic events are influenced by the presence of measuring devices and, in that sense, by the presence of observers) became occult dogma.

The alienation in the society was mirrored by the tradition in those books of identifying a surname by just the first letter, a Kafkaesque touch: Joseph K. as an astral traveler. This technique created a faceless flat presence like the false front of a building on a movie set. Only the suggestion of reality.

By mid-century, the out-of-the-body phenomenon, as suspect as phrenology and UFOs, had been abandoned by serious parapsychologists, who were wary of the subject because of its occult taint. Getting recognition for their ESP experiments was hard enough without dragging in astral bodies. So they stuck to flipping cards and rolling dice, teasing out significance from statistical improbability and offering as evidence of extrasensory perception cases in which subjects succeeded in identifying the symbols on hidden cards or in predicting the roll of dice more often than they would be expected to —according to probability theory—if they were guessing.

But anomalously the change in the intellectual climate of parapsychology started at the same time the out-of-the-body experience had been surrendered to the occultists. In the early 1950s interest in Oriental mysticism and the mind-altering properties of certain chemicals and plants had begun percolating through a culture in America which was both exhilarated by and terrified of the triumphant materialism that had, among other accomplishments, created the atomic bomb. (In cartoons, nuclear fission was repeatedly portrayed as a sinister genie who, barely controlled by the Aladdins at the Atomic Energy Commission, was ready to give us a sultan's comfort or leave us in only the rags of our flesh.) LSD-25, a hallucinogenic drug derived from ergot, a fungus that grows on rye and wheat, was accidentally discovered in 1943 by a Swiss chemist, Dr. Albert Hoffman, who reported, according to Owen S. Rachleff in *The Occult Conceit,* that the drug had given him a feeling of "being outside my body"—and, by the early fifties, the drug was being used to create what seemed to be laboratory psychoses, Arabian Nights fantasies in the minds of selected guinea pigs. In 1954 Aldous Huxley published *The Doors of Perception,* in which he gave an account of the experiences he'd had the previous spring after having swallowed four-tenths of a gram of mescaline, an alkaloid isolated in 1896, which is the active principle of the hallucinogenic peyote cactus. He described the feeling that his senses, having been skinned, were receiving unblocked perceptions of what was *out there* in objective reality. In the same year, a paperback edition of the *Bhagavad-Gita*, translated by Swami Prabhavananda and Christopher Isherwood, was published, the first of many reincarnations the book would have as it went from one printing which sold out to another. The Baynes-Wilhelm translation of the *I Ching*, a book that would become the Gideon Bible of many communes, had by 1955 gone into its third printing since the original two-volume edition had appeared in April of 1950. Alan Watts and D. T. Suzuki were interpreting Eastern philosophy to the Beats and Bohemians, who within ten years would reinterpret it to a generation which would get much of its Buddhism filtered through the apocalypses of Allen Ginsberg and the gentle ecology of Gary Snyder.

So among intellectuals the rigid habits of materialism were already under assault in 1952, when Dr. Hornell Hart, a professor of sociology at Duke University, asked forty-two students: "Have you ever actually seen your physical body from a viewpoint completely outside that body, like standing *beside* the bed and looking at yourself lying *in* the bed, or like floating in the air near your body?" According to his paper, "ESP Projection: Spontaneous Cases and the Experimental Method," which was published in *The Journal of the American Society for Psychical Research* (Vol. XLVIII, No. 4, October, 1954), one-third of those asked said yes. The paper also described the results of a previous sampling of another group of one hundred and thirteen students, whom Hart had asked: "Have you ever dreamed of standing outside your body or floating in the air near your body?" Of those students, 24.8 per cent answered yes.

Hart, who was born on August 2, 1888, in St. Paul, Minnesota, received his B.A. from Oberlin College in Ohio, his M.A. from the University of Wisconsin in Madison, and his Ph.D. from the State University of Iowa in Iowa City—a peripatetic scholar. After having taught for nearly a decade at Bryn Mawr College in Pennsylvania and for half a decade at the Hartford Theological Seminary in Connecticut, in 1938 he went to Duke University, where he became involved in the experiments being carried out at Dr. J. B. Rhine's famous Parapsychological Laboratory, at a time when it was risky for a serious academic to work in psychical research. Using sociological methods, he helped develop a scientific approach to parapsychology; and, by the time he died in 1967, parapsychology, the prodigal child of nineteenth century rationalism, was being welcomed, partly as a result of his efforts, into the academic fold.

In December, 1969, after a sponsoring speech by Dr. Margaret Mead, the American Academy for the Advancement of Science voted 165 to 30 in favor of admitting the Parapsychological Association, an international organization, founded in 1957, which had at the time of its admission to the AAAS a membership of about two hundred researchers from twenty-five countries.

Within five years after Hart's death, parapsychology had a secure purchase on the intellectual imagination of the last third of the twentieth century. By the beginning of the 1970s, one hundred American colleges and universities offered courses in psychical research—according to *Time*, which, devoting its March 4, 1974, cover story to parapsychology, reflected America's nervous interest in a subject that, as a result of both research and fashion, was becoming as difficult to ignore as it was to accept. In 1972 the United States National Institute of Mental Health granted the Dream Laboratory at Maimonides Medical Center in Brooklyn, New York, $52,000 to continue its experiments with telepathy—government funding, the final benison of our society. And a poll taken that year in the November 23 issue of the professionally irreproachable British magazine *New Scientist* disclosed that eighty-eight per cent of the 1252 readers whose replies were tabulated believed psychical research was a legitimate undertaking. Twenty-five per cent believed ESP was "an established fact."

So the shock of academic acceptance, combined with the increasing enthusiasm in the culture for Oriental mysticism and mind-altering drugs, freed parapsychological researchers to probe comfortably into previously suspect subjects like out-of-the-body phenomena.

According to a paper written by Hart shortly before his death for the March, 1967, issue of *The International Journal of Parapsychology*, "more than 400 cases [of out-of-the-body experiences], classified and fairly well analyzed, had been published" between 1961 and 1965.

In September, 1966, Celia Green, director of the Institute of Psychophysical Research (an independent parapsychological think-tank in a Victorian house about a twenty-minute walk from Oxford University in England), advertised in the press and on radio for people who had experienced out-of-the-body states. After correlating her approximately four hundred replies with the information gathered from two follow-up questionnaires, she revealed in *Out-of-the-Body Experiences,* a slim statistic-gorged corporation-report of a book published in 1968, that, according to her sample population, people tended to have out-of-the-body experiences lying down three times more frequently than when they were sitting, that approximately twenty per cent of those who left their bodies did so six times or more, and that in out-of-the-body states sight dominated. The disembodied consciousness slighted the other senses. Hearing, touch, smell, taste, like rungs on a ladder descending to oblivion, were described respectively less and less often.

And in the March-April, 1972, issue of the *Parapsychology Review,* Dr. J. C. Poynton, professor of biological science at the University of Natal, Durban, South Africa, published the results of a fifteen-item questionnaire which he had run in South Africa's *Sunday Times* and in the Zulu newspaper *Ilanga lase Natal* and which he had distributed to the Bantu and Indian communities in South Africa. After correlating the one hundred and twenty-two responses he received, he found that seventy-six per cent of the episodes

> occurred during a state of physical relaxation. . . . Sixty-five per cent of the experiences occurred without any previous knowledge of OOB experiences. . . . Seventy-six per cent of the experiences involved "some body or form that you could distinctly see or feel" . . . [and] twenty-seven per cent of the cases appeared to give external confirmation of the reality of the experience. . . .

"There are immense problems involved in studying a subject like the out-of-the-body phenomenon," said Mrs. Jerald Tickell, editor of the British *Journal of the Society for Psychical Research.* She sat in her cluttered office at the Society's headquarters in London at 1 Adam and Eve Mews, an appropriate address, considering parapsychologists' innocence of the principles behind psychic phenomena. As she talked, she moved her hands over the desk in front of her as though she were picking up and putting down a small invisible box. "It's easy enough collecting cases. You run across them every day. Not too long ago, my secretary told me of an experience her boyfriend, a racing driver, had. And it's easy enough correlating the cases once you get them. How many women, how many men, how many children have the experience. That's important, but it's not enough.

"I rather suspect that out-of-the-body experiences are some form of clairvoyance, but we'll never know unless we find new ways of approaching the subject. How do you organize the cases so they make sense, so they're not just facts left up in the air? And how do you deal with the phenomenon in the laboratory? If a subject can't have an out-of-the-body experience on command, then it's very difficult to check whether or not the experience is real; and, if the subject can easily duplicate the experiences, then you don't want to trust him, do you, since the experience by its nature tends to be spontaneous. . . .

"What we need," she said, looking down at the space between her hands, as though she could find some answers within the imaginary box she held, "are good researchers who can produce convincing, meaningful data under controlled laboratory conditions."

PART 2

ADEPTS IN THE LABORATORY

There was a time when I thought a great deal about the axolotls. I went to see them in the aquarium at the Jardins des Plantes and stayed for hours watching them, observing their immobility, their faint movements. . . . My face was pressed against the glass of the aquarium. . . . I saw from up close the face of an axolotl immobile next to the glass. No transition and no surprise, I saw my face against the glass, I saw it on the outside of the tank, I saw it on the other side of the glass. Then my face drew back and I understood . . . I was an axolotl.

JULIO CORTAZAR, *"Axolotl"*

CHAPTER 5

Outside The Glass

ON JUNE 30, 1966, Dr. Stanley Krippner, director of the Dream Laboratory at Maimonides Medical Center in Brooklyn, New York, was monitoring an ESP-dream experiment with a student whom he called Jim U. (The impulse to strip away the personal face, protecting privacy, transforming the individual into an impersonal subject, is as strong in parapsychology as it is in the occult.) The test was routine, part of a series the Dream Laboratory had been conducting since 1964.

Each subject was wired to an electroencephalograph before he went to sleep. Agents in another room would try to send telepathically the image of an art reproduction which had been picked randomly from a pool of possible targets. Whenever the electroencephalograph indicated possible dream activity, the monitor would wake the subject and question him about his dreams.

The results from the series of tests had been encouraging; there was evidence that some form of ESP did exist. And, although Jim had told Krippner that on occasion he had the sensation of leaving his body, Krippner was absorbed in testing for telepathy, not out-of-the-body experiences.

In one experiment Krippner woke Jim about ten minutes after the first sign that his subject was dreaming. Jim said he had been dreaming of a club where he worked as a life guard. Kids were running around, and he talked to a life guard who was standing by the swimming pool. The experience was distinct and very real. Not an extraordinary dream, but the next morning Jim told Krippner that just before the dream started he had felt the beginning of an out-of-the-body experience, a sensation of being cranked up that lasted about forty-five seconds. As soon as he realized that he was on the verge of the experience, he became aware of where he was and why, and that awareness smothered the feelings that his consciousness was about to leave his body. He woke up, unhappy that he had failed to generate a complete out-of-the-body episode.

Intrigued, Krippner began watching for a more successful repetition of Jim's out-of-the-body experience; other members of the staff were alerted to the possibility. On August 11 and August 18 after ESP-dream experiments, monitors asked Jim if he'd had any out-of-the-body sensations; but Jim's consciousness seemed anchored to his body, and the Dream Laboratory returned its attention to telepathy.

"It was frustrating," said Krippner seven years later in his office at the Maimonides Dream Laboratory, which had been recently renamed the Division of Parapsychology and Psychophysics in an attempt to describe more accurately that curious hybrid field. "Our short stab at experimenting with out-of-the-body experiments was one of the first studies of its type. But we had to give it up because we had no guarantee that our subject would have an out-of-the-body experience, and the work here is so expensive."

Krippner was the first scientific researcher I spoke to about the phenomenon, and he was a serious, responsible man, educated at the University of Wisconsin and Northwestern University. But talking to him gave me a feeling of dislocation, of being unbalanced, as though I were trying to walk a straight line in a carnival funhouse where the perspectives were wrong and the floor was slightly tilted.

He chatted confidently about telepathy, comparing it to the out-of-the-body experience: "I think we have good evidence for telepathy; but while that may be important for studies on out-of-the-body states, we can't be sure. We don't know whether during an out-of-the-body state the subject is experiencing a form of ESP or whether something actually separates from the body."

Because Krippner's out-of-the-body experiment had been aborted, he could only speculate tentatively on the nature of the phenomenon; but to me, new to parapsychological research, even his cautious musings —the fact that he even entertained the notion that in an out-of-the-body experience some part of consciousness might really leave the physical self—seemed preposterous.

I was left with the intimation that perhaps studying such a subject from the outside would be like trying to describe the atmosphere of a selective club by standing on a noisy street and peering up at the sedate interior through half-draped windows. Although Krippner said, "I suspect strongly that it is something which can be studied in a laboratory situation," I was not convinced. It seemed too much like trying to prove the existence of the soul by excavating the flesh. What were the limits to the scientific method? Could you flatten God between two glass slides, tint Him, and squint through a microscope at the universe in His captured tissue? If one of the skirmishes between mysticism and rationalism was being carried on in the field of out-of-the-body research, scientists who seriously examined the subject must be fifth columnists for the occult.

Disappointed with this first interview and prejudging the other interviews I had arranged—a circuit through the psychic community—I left Krippner, confident that any study of the out-of-the-body experience could only be an alchemy in which external objects were manipulated to produce internal changes. Not science, revelation. Things, however, turned out to be not that simple.

CHAPTER 6

In The Vortex

IN THE SAME YEAR that Stanley Krippner was tentatively exploring Jim U.'s out-of-the-body abilities in Brooklyn, the University of Virginia Department of Psychiatry established their Division of Parapsychology. The project was funded by a bequest of one million dollars from the estate of Chester F. Carlson, the inventor of the Xerox process, who left equal amounts to the American Society for Psychical Research and to Dr. J. B. Rhine's Foundation for Research on the Nature of Man. Under the direction of Dr. Ian Stevenson, the former chairman of the University of Virginia's Department of Psychiatry, the Division of Parapsychology began studying reincarnation and out-of-the-body experiences, two subjects that parapsychologists had been uneasy dealing with.

"There are three approaches you could take to the

study of out-of-the-body experiences," said Dr. John Palmer, a research associate in the Division of Parapsychology.

Slight, balding, in his thirties, Palmer leaned forward over his desk in his office in the renovated red brick house in which the Division of Parapsychology had its library and laboratories. As he spoke, he touched his fingers along the edge of the desk as though he were playing the piano, about to strike music from the wood with a parapsychologist's spell. He paused frequently to modify what he had just said, to plot what he would say, measuring his words with the care of a chemist preparing an explosive potion.

"You can collect and analyze spontaneous cases, people who have had one or two experiences in their lives. But you never get good data that way. You have to get the cases from advertising, and then you have the problem of deciding if your sample is representative of the population at large. You may have more women than men sending in cases, for example, simply because they have more time to do it. If you weren't careful, you'd be led to a conclusion that the experience is more common in women, when it probably is not. In fact, that conclusion has been drawn by some researchers.

"Or you can work with people who have multiple experiences. But you run into two problems there. First, anyone who has frequent out-of-the-body experiences may not be a typical case, and so any conclusions you may draw can't be safely generalized. Second, unless you find someone who can control his experiences, you end up hoping that he'll happen to have an experience while he's in the laboratory, which usually doesn't happen because of the tension and distraction and a number of other factors that might get in the way.

"The ideal way to study out-of-the-body experiences would be to develop a repeatable experiment that uses a random population."

Palmer's interest in parapsychology was triggered in the early sixties while he was an undergraduate at Duke University in Durham, North Carolina, where Dr. J. B. Rhine had been studying telepathy and clairvoyance since 1930 and where Dr. Hornell Hart had carried out his out-of-the-body experience survey in 1952.

Out of curiosity Palmer visited Rhine's Parapsychology Laboratory and on a few occasions was a subject in the experiments. Since Palmer was a major in psychology, specializing in personality, parapsychology —a field struggling for professional acceptance—must have had the same attraction for him that well-written pornography has for the serious English major. When he needed a part-time job in the summer of 1966 after he had graduated, he approached Rhine, who, after leaving Duke in 1965, had set up his Foundation for Research on the Nature of Man in Durham, near the university.

Palmer worked at Rhine's foundation for two summers, but did not have another chance to do serious parapsychological research until, having received his doctorate in experimental psychology from the University of Texas at Austin and having taught for two years at McGill University in Montreal, Canada, he came to the University of Virginia in Charlottesville.

In June of 1973 Palmer began a series of experiments in which he tried to induce out-of-the-body experiences in student volunteers from the University of Virginia by first having them relax (using a technique called the Jacobson Method of repeatedly tensing and releasing the muscles) and then placing them in a disorienting environment, a dark room where they listened to a 350 Hz. sine wave tone with a frequency oscillation of ± 5 Hz.—a high-pitched *hwha hwha hwha*—while staring at a rotating eighteen-inch fluorescent moire disk which had on its face a spiral that appeared to go into and away from its center and was illuminated by a strobe light passed through a black light filter: a research style that seemed to owe as much to the midsixties psychedelia of San Francisco's Avalon Ballroom as to the experimental psychologist's laboratory.

"The disk was rotated at approximately 1200 RPM," said Palmer, "but by adjusting the frequency of the strobe light it could be made to look like it was rotating at any speed or in any direction the subject desired. And we had two sources of sound—out of a cassette tape recorder and out of headphones the subject was wearing. We could modulate the amplitude of what was coming through the headphones, but not what was coming through the speaker. This produced a numbing effect."

The students were asked to imagine themselves leaving their bodies after they had bathed for nine minutes in this vortex of light and noise, which Palmer hoped would suck their consciousnesses from their flesh and deposit them, like Dorothy after the tornado, in some psychic Oz. Of fifty students tested, forty-two per cent said they had felt that they were at some point during the experiment literally outside their physical bodies.

"The strongest reaction," Palmer said, "was of a subject who saw what seemed to be an apparition of his body at the door of the laboratory and then realized that his consciousness was in that apparitional body, looking back at his physical body.

"The out-of-the-body experience seemed to be a two-stage process. The feeling of disorientation induced by various stimuli triggered the apparition, and then the apparition provided the explanation for the sensations of dissociation from his physical body that he felt."

Like primitive man, we create myths to help explain confusing facts: if it thunders, there must be a thunder-god, a risky method of deduction that Western science —in a more sophisticated form—has strapped itself to. Everything depends on the premise, so the act of identifying the proposition from which you will draw your conclusions becomes as significant as driving a piton into a rock face you're climbing.

Palmer's star subject had rationalized his feelings of disorientation and dissociation from his physical body by accepting a logic which allowed him to believe that consciousness could operate free of the body. My more earth-bound logic said it couldn't. And I was unprepared to negotiate between these two opposing views. So I was contented with Palmer's approach to the phenomenon, which was to treat an out-of-the-body episode as only a subjective event. The perceived experience was illusionary; it was the feeling that was real.

"There may be nothing paranormal about the out-of-the-body experience," Palmer said, "although a number of people who have had the experience are quite sure they really were out, and the arguments I might put forth about how our minds can play tricks on us aren't very convincing to them. The only real fact you have—what you must begin with—is that the sensation of being outside the body is real. It can't be dismissed as, say, a dream, although it may have elements in it which are related to dream states. It is a separate phenomenon. The thing that distinguishes the out-of-the-body experience from a dream or a fantasy is the *proprioceptive* aspect—what you feel, the conviction that you really have separated from the physical body. When the experience is over, you don't think, 'Well, it wasn't real after all. . . .' "

But Palmer used the subjective reality of the experience, like a plank laid on quicksand, to probe into the paranormal.

"What we're not sure of is whether the reality of the experience goes beyond that subjective sensation, whether some aspect of the self really does separate from the body."

Evidence for ESP gathered during an out-of-the-body episode does not prove that the out-of-the-body feeling is something more than a subjective sensation because whatever ESP seems to occur during an out-of-the-body experience may have only a coincidental relationship to the experience itself.

"ESP and the sightings of a second body that are sometimes reported in an out-of-the-body experience may—if they are authentic—merely be extraordinary events that happen to occur at the same time someone feels he is out of his body," said Palmer.

Because Palmer probed judiciously, I found, by the end of my visit with him, that I had strayed farther into the unknown than I had expected to. I had swallowed Palmer's casual "if they are authentic" as easily as if it had been an oyster undunked in hot sauce. "If they are authentic" gave the nod to a crowd of ideas I had previously withstood. By entertaining the subjunctive, Palmer fused my disbelief in the objective reality of the out-of-the-body experience to his star subject's belief in it and produced a paradoxical synthesis which I kept discovering in other forms throughout the rest of my investigation: "I'm not sure if my view of the out-of-the-body experience—that it is subjective, an internally generated experience—is necessarily contradictory to the notion that the person may actually leave his body."

CHAPTER 7

Robert Morris

IN THE MID-1960s, while an undergraduate psychology major at Duke University, John Palmer met Robert Morris, a doctoral student in biological psychology at Duke, who was also curious about psychic phenonena and who, like Palmer, spent summers working at Rhine's Foundation for Research on the Nature of Man.

When I met Morris in 1973, he was coordinator of the out-of-the-body experience project at the Psychical Research Foundation in Durham, North Carolina, an organization with offices and laboratories in three buildings which are near both the campus of Duke University and the Foundation for Research on the Nature of Man.

"Long before I got to Duke, I was involved in parapsychology," he told me. "My parents had been very interested in psychic phenomena. When they were dating before they got married, they had a friend who appeared to have some mediumistic abilities, and they attended a seance where they were convinced they had contacted a deceased friend. They communicated their interest to me."

But Morris's interest focused on the seen, not the unseen. Rather than listen to the murmur of the dead, he experimented with a toy for testing ESP that another friend of his parents had developed: a box with a hopper on top which held twenty-five differently colored marbles. When you turned a knob, one marble dropped down into the box behind a clear plastic window on the side, and by trying to guess (before looking) what color the marble was you could check your ESP ability. A crude device but, according to Morris, "It made the abstract aspects of psychical phenomena specific for me, and by the time I was fourteen I was testing all my friends."

Morris talked with his eyes wide opened and his eyebrows arched as though he were permanently surprised by what he studied. He took the ESP-testing box, which he had saved, from the top of the desk in his office at the Psychical Research Foundation and demonstrated how it worked.

"While I was at the University of Pittsburgh, I tried the box on a friend, a philosophy major I used to argue with, who didn't believe in psychic phenomena, and he didn't guess any of the twenty-five marbles correctly, which is a negatively meaningful result. According to chance, he should have gotten some right.

"This is really what kept me interested in parapsychology: the fact that people resist any investigation of the phenomena which, who knows, may or may not be paranormal, but which certainly raise questions."

At the University of Pittsburgh, Morris was encouraged to follow up his interest in parapsychology by Dr. Robert McConnell, a biophysicist and a former president of the Parapsychological Association. After receiving his B.A. in psychology in 1963, Morris went to Duke where he got his Ph.D. in 1969. He completed postdoctoral work at Duke's Center for the Study of Aging and Human Development, and in 1971 he joined the staff of the Psychical Research Foundation as full-time project coordinator.

Until 1971 the Psychical Research Foundation had been struggling along on the modest bequest left to the organization by Charles Eugene Ozanne. A former Harvard College history instructor and public school teacher from Cleveland, Ohio, Ozanne helped to support psychical research at Duke in the 1930s and in 1959 approached Dr. Rhine about creating a center for research on the soul-survival question. With Rhine's help, Ozanne organized the Psychical Research Foundation during the year before he died; and, once the new foundation was established, Rhine asked William Roll, at the time a research associate at Duke's Parapsychological Laboratory, to become the foundation's director of research. Roll received his B.A. from the University of California in 1949 and his B. Litt. from Oxford University in 1960; from 1952 to 1957, while at Oxford, he was president of the Oxford University Society for Psychical Research.

When Morris came to the Psychical Research Foundation, Roll had just completed successful negotiations with the Parapsychological Foundation for a sizable grant (part of which went to help pay Morris's salary), and the Psychical Research Foundation was in the midst of a six-year court battle over distribution of

$270,000 left for soul-survival research by James Kidd, an Arizona prospector who vanished in 1949 when he was 71 years old. On December 29, 1972, the Superior Court of Maricopa County, Arizona, ruled that Kidd's entire estate be left to the American Society for Psychical Research; but the ASPR generously let it be known that they would look with favor on any reasonable project proposal submitted by the Psychical Research Foundation.

Morris and Roll outlined a series of experiments for studying both out-of-the-body experiences and alleged cases of hauntings, an intellectual pincer movement designed to trap man's disembodied consciousness either in this world or the next. The ASPR agreed to fund their research.

As part of the strategy for catching the disembodied self, the Psychical Research Foundation developed a model of consciousness which placed the out-of-the-body experience into one narrow band on the spectrum of mind activity that shrinks into the ultraviolet of pure egoism on one end and disappears into the infrared of totally expanded consciousness, a merging with the All, on the other end. Their model made them *neo*-Neoplatonists, because it mirrored Plotinus's conception of a self which can skid from normal consciousness to a "self-encentered" ecstasy to a perfect union with the One.

In the proposal explaining his research intentions, Roll used the phrase *transpersonal consciousness* (TC) to describe all experiences in which one feels that consciousness has somehow transcended the physical body. He also identified two questions of prime importance to any investigation of transpersonal consciousness. First, how real are states of transpersonal consciousness; and, second, how independent is a consciousness that seems to have transcended the physical body?

Although Roll's proposal flirted with the soul-survival question (in deference to both the charter of the Psychical Research Foundation and the stipulations in James Kidd's will), the out-of-the-body experience studies done by the Psychical Research Foundation concentrated only on that part of the consciousness which is an aspect of the living subject. The proposal indicated interest in all transpersonal states, but Morris—navigating neatly between the grave and godhood—limited his research to out-of-the-body states.

Morris began his study of out-of-the-body experiences in January, 1973. The experiments were designed to probe for three kinds of evidence which the out-of-the-body experience, if real, could produce. The subject's psychophysiological responses (brain-wave patterns, heart beat, respiration rate) were monitored while he claimed to be in the out-of-the-body state and were compared to the results of similar tests carried out while he was dreaming, meditating, imagining having an out-of-the-body flight, or about to have what he considered to be a real out-of-the-body episode. His responses to the targets prepared for him in another room or in another building were recorded to see whether or not he could correctly identify objects he was asked to perceive while he was in the out-of-the-body state. And the activities of various detectors (humans, kittens, devices for measuring changes in electromagnetic field strength, in temperature, in energy levels) were watched, while the subject tried to affect the detectors in his out-of-the-body state.

"At first we had a little difficulty finding subjects we could work with," said Morris. "We wanted to avoid

anyone who lived too far away. We didn't like the awk-
ward interaction of having someone come here for two
weeks on a put-up-or-shut-up basis. We wanted to avoid
any subject who had an extensive psychiatric or drug
history, for obvious reasons. We wanted to avoid anyone who would place the out-of-the-body experience in
an emotionally powerful religious context. We wanted
to work only with people who were fully prepared for
the possibility that the experiments would be nothing
more than very interesting and perhaps potentially
useful forms of mental exercise.

"We also wanted to work with people who were comfortable with the experience, so we wouldn't have to go
through any growing pains with them. We wanted the
experiments to be relaxed. We wanted to be able to say
to our subject, 'Twice a week we'd like you to come in
and spend an evening with us and have a couple of
oobies.' "

And, of course, Morris wanted subjects who could
control their out-of-the-body experiences. Of the
people he interviewed, fewer than a dozen seemed
to be serious prospects. At one point he decided to
experiment with a couple, who, in a psychic Jack-
Spratt-and-wife team, had out-of-the-body episodes
alternately: he left his body before sleep; she left her
body before waking. But in the laboratory situation
they suffered from experimental stage fright, staying
within their bodies like nervous actors who hang
back in the wings.

"Even when some of the people we screened were
finally able to have *oobies,* they seemed to be limited
in some way," Morris said. "They may have had no
trouble getting out of their bodies, for example, but
they weren't able to leave the room where their bodies

were sitting. They were bound by what seemed to be only psychological constraints."

Certain subjects seemed to create for their out-of-the-body worlds rules which they could not violate, as though, once created, the rules developed a reality of their own.

"This wasn't satisfactory. For the tidiness of the kind of questions we wanted to ask, we wanted people to be able to take a trip from a room in a psychophysical lab at Duke, which is about a quarter of a mile away, to a room in one of our buildings. That way we wouldn't have to worry about accidental leakage of information. We used electronic clocks in both places, so all activity, both of the subject and the target detectors, was synchronized."

Morris finally decided to work with a twenty-year-old undergraduate psychology major at Duke University, Blue Harary, who claimed to have had out-of-the-body experiences ever since he was a child, and who was the most convincing adept I spoke to during my research in the psychic underground.

CHAPTER 8

Blue

PEOPLE WHO HAVE WORKED with Blue Harary tend to describe him in legendary terms as visible proof of the reality of the out-of-the-body phenomenon. He is presented as the personification of the experience, a psychical Paul Bunyan. When I met him, I felt both awed and cynical—appropriate feelings in the presence of a myth. It was easier for me to believe in Blue's power to leave his body than it was for me to believe in the same power of, say, Abaris, because Blue was present, obviously real himself and very convincing. It was also harder for me to believe in Blue's power to leave his body than it was for me to believe in the reports of Abaris's power, because Blue's physical presence inhibited me from recreating him in my imagination.

Blue was born Stuart Harary on February 9, 1953, at Maimonides Hospital in Brooklyn, New York—in the same medical center in which the Dream Laboratory was established a decade later.

"I grew up on Long Island," he said. "East Meadow, out in Hempstead, near Levittown."

He gave the four geographical coordinates as though they would also locate him socially and economically. His family was middle class, suburban; his parents were Orthodox Jews who, too busy for elaborate ritual, became Conservative by default.

As he described his childhood, he created the scenes in the air with his hands. Occasionally, he paused to rethink a sentence, as though he had stopped a tape in his head and was rewinding it so he could play it through again to check for mistakes.

When he was about six years old, he claimed, he discovered what he described as discarnate friends. They were not the imaginary playmates that most kids invent, Blue insisted; or, if they were the same, then those imaginary playmates kids have are real, because Blue's discarnate friends repeatedly gave him information about relatives' deaths, schoolmates' sicknesses, family crises—none of which he would have had any way of knowing about because the events had happened somewhere else or hadn't taken place yet.

One night while riding in his parents' car back from Brooklyn, his discarnate friends told him, "Look out the front window. Watch the lights along the side of the highway."

Blue, kneeling up in the front seat, did as they suggested. Whenever a car coming up behind them flashed its headlights into their car, he saw the reflection of his family in the curved glass of the windshield.

"Now, keep looking," the discarnate friends told him. He concentrated on the lights beside the highway, which snapped past, appearing to speed up like a movie running faster and faster, until the lights became white blurs. The landscape blurred. His family blurred. And the world, by blurring, suddenly came into focus, as though two realities existed at the same time within the same space and, whenever he concentrated on one, the other one faded.

"You're seeing things differently than the people around you are seeing them," said his discarnate friends. "That's what you're going to have to do from now on."

"O.K.," said Blue, not quite sure what was going on, aware only that he was experiencing the world with more intensity, perceiving things with more attention, as though time had slowed and he were able to examine what was occurring around him in a leisurely fashion. If he stared at an object, all his other senses seemed to click off, and his consciousness seemed to dwindle in his body at the same time that it became clearer and sharper at a point outside of his body.

During recess in elementary school, Blue would sit on a hill under a tree, listening to the sounds from the playground, the thud of a kicked ball or the crack of a ball against a bat, the screams of the kids, the voice of the teacher calling above the noise—calling, often, to Blue, urging him to play with the group. His classmates teased him, challenging him to play ball with them; and, when he refused, they beat him.

"Along about the eighth grade," Blue said, "I demanded the right to be me, and not to have to do what everybody else did. Not to have to feel the way they did. Things were just getting worse and worse. I wasn't feeling good about myself."

Blue discussed his unhappy childhood experiences

dispassionately, distanced from the pain by time and karate. He felt no need of self-pity, since he had learned to defend himself against his tormentors. But after using karate on a few occasions, he abandoned it, unwilling to be forced to choose between being villain or victim.

When he was about fourteen, he was lying one night on his bed in his room in the basement of his parents' house. It was, as he preferred, completely dark. Just as he was falling asleep, he realized that his consciousness was floating two feet above his body, which had gone rigid on the bed.

There was a wall to his right, a lamp hanging above his head, and to his left (the "sinister" side that is considered in many mythologies the side on which death waits) was a large, dark, disembodied hulking figure without features. A silhouette, but not a shadow.

"I heard this grunting, like breathing," said Blue, "which may have been, now that I think of it, the physical body underneath me, not that creature, whatever it was, on the other side of the room. It moved closer. It really terrified me. It was very bad. I felt it wanted to do me some harm. My physical body couldn't move. The thing was getting closer. It was right near the bed. I tried to get all my energy into this hand, my right hand—which might be significant because I use my left hand to write—and I reached up and grabbed the chain on the lamp, yanked it down, practically broke the thing I pulled so hard. I just thought the light would do something. I felt a jolt, and everything was all right. I was sitting there in the light, trying to figure out what had happened. I was back in my body.

"But the light didn't scare the thing away. When I made the sudden movement, I snapped back into my body, so I couldn't perceive it anymore. But I was sure it was still there."

For a long time after that experience Blue refused to sleep with the light off. He didn't understand what had happened, but he didn't want the experience—whatever it was—to happen again.

Shortly afterward, on his birthday, around midnight —the hour he was born—Blue was sitting tipped back in a chair in his room, listening to "Unhappy Girl" by Jim Morrison and The Doors. To unkink his muscles, he stretched. As he was relaxing, he felt himself dissolve into another world. He was aware of his physical body still sitting, tipped back in the chair, but his consciousness was positioned somewhere in front of it. And he had a vague sense of other beings, like the discarnate friends he'd had as a child. One of those disembodied beings said, "You have to keep going. . . . You have something to learn. . . ."

Images and sounds spun by him; and when he glanced up at the clock, he was back in his body, a pain in his solar plexus as though someone had slugged him in the belly with a club. He was sure only a few minutes had gone by, but it was five o'clock in the morning. Five hours had passed.

He did not tell his family about the odd episodes. As he was growing up, they occurred more and more often, sometimes accompanied by telepathic or precognitive phenomena. While an undergraduate at Nebraska Wesleyan University in Lincoln, he had an out-of-the-body experience during which he had an insistent but formless impression that his parents should not drive their car. He called them, slyly led the conversation around to the state of the car. Yes, his parents admitted, the car had been acting funny.

Maybe they should get it checked before they drove it, Blue suggested. They said they would. When they brought it into a garage, they were told that the axle was about to break.

During one of his out-of-the-body episodes, Blue, responding to some unexplained prompting, asked one of his discarnate friends, "What's my name?"

Blue explained: "It seemed like a weird question to ask, and they said 'Blue.' Like, 'That's a crazy question. Of course you should have known that already. That's your name.'"

Late in 1971 Blue came home to New York on vacation. While visiting the Museum of Natural History, he decided to investigate the American Society for Psychical Research, which was only six blocks away. When he called, the receptionist at the society said they were just about to close and only one researcher was in the building. Blue asked if he could rush over anyway; the receptionist agreed.

When Blue arrived, he introduced himself to the lone researcher, Janet Mitchell, who was setting up an out-of-the-body experiment. She asked how he had gotten interested in psychical research, and Blue cautiously said, "Well, I've had a couple of strange experiences that I can't explain."

"Telepathy?" she asked.

"Yeah," said Blue. "Sometimes. And others."

"Out-of-the-body experiences?" she asked, a random question. She was working in the field, and the phenomenon was on her mind.

"Yeah," said Blue. "Sometimes."

"Now, I'd never heard the term before," Blue said, "but just by the name I knew exactly what she was talking about. I looked at her; she looked at me.

" 'Well,' she said, 'we're doing research in it. Do you want to experiment?'

"I said, 'No,' because I wasn't sure of the situation there yet."

But a few months later Blue returned to the American Society for Psychical Research. When Janet introduced him to Dr. Karlis Osis, research director at the society, Osis said, "Ah-ha, wouldn't you know it; we have an experiment all set up. Why don't you come up and do it?"

Blue was supposed to extend his consciousness upstairs into a room he had never been in before, spot a target, return, and describe what he had perceived.

"I saw a lot of stuff," Blue told Janet, when his consciousness had returned to his body. "A rectangular box with wires, and on front of that a circle with an X in it. A statuette. And antlers."

Blue kept repeating, "antlers." Janet, excited that Blue had felt the experiment was successful, led him upstairs to check on the targets, which she had not previously seen either. Blue felt embarrassed by the whole procedure; he was not sure what he believed about his out-of-the-body experiences. A projection could be only imagination; and even if part of the out-of-the-body experience were authentic, Blue didn't know how much of what happened during the episodes was valid because at that point he had no real control of his consciousness when it seemed to be out of his body. Once, during the experiment, he had found himself on the street outside the society's headquarters; later in the experiment he had found himself in the subway.

When they got upstairs, Osis showed them the targets: a rectangular tape recorder with wires running

out of it and a circular reel on top, which, like most tape
reels, had an X cut out of the plastic to reveal how much
of the tape was wound; next to the tape recorder there
was a statuette of a reindeer with large antlers.

During the following summer, Blue worked with the
American Society for Psychical Research as a subject in
their out-of-the-body experiments, and in September
he transferred to Duke University so he could participate in the out-of-the-body studies at the Psychical Research Foundation.

On the days Blue engaged in Morris's experiments,
he would wander mildly from event to event, sidestep-
ping any crisis, trying to avoid emotional distractions.
An hour before the sessions, which usually took place
after dark, Blue would bathe and meditate. Just before
the experiments he would "cool down" by using the
Jacobson method which Palmer also used on his subjects at the University of Virginia.

Wired like a puppet to a 12-channel Grass polygraph,
Blue would be closed in a soundproof room which was
completely dark. All he could hear would be the blank
monotony of a white noise background, the emotionless
tone in which gods and sibyls speak to man.

At a certain point, he reported, he'd find himself
losing control, slipping from his body. While he would
attempt to extend his consciousness into the target
room, the polygraph would be monitoring his respiration rate, his vasomotor activity (whether his blood ves-
sels were dilating or constricting), his skin resistance
(which would indicate how aroused he was), his eye
movements, his left and right occipital electroenceph-
alogram (EEG), and his muscle tone. These various psychophysiological measurements were also taken for
imaginary out-of-the-body experiences, when Blue

would fantasize the sensations of being out of his body without actually having the authentic experience.

The results of the psychophysiological monitoring were inconclusive, although Morris found that Blue's respiration and heart rates increased to a significant degree and his skin potential decreased to a significant degree while he was experiencing the sensations of being out of his body. Morris also found that, while Blue was in the out-of-the-body state, there were significant changes in his vasomotor activity and his eye movement seemed to slow, but these responses were not as consistent as the increases in respiration and heart rates and the decrease in skin potential. From these results Morris concluded that Blue's out-of-the-body state was physiologically distinct from both his "cool down" state or the typical rapid-eye-movement dream state.

In the response-to-target tests Morris had Blue try to identify the location of people spaced around the target room and to report on colored letters which were hung on the walls.

"The first two times we used the location of people," said Morris, "he got everything right. The results then declined, a pattern common to most kinds of psychic experiments. The subject gets interested in doing something and succeeds in doing it. Then his interest lags, and the results drop off. Although there's not very much evidence to go on, this decline could indicate some relationship between out-of-the-body experiences and ESP.

"Blue didn't do well with the colored letters either. Sometimes he'd seem to have the letter rotated; a Z might be perceived as an N. Sometimes he would make a correct hit. But I'd be hesitant to claim any success for that aspect of the project."

"When you're out of your body," said Blue, "sometimes things seem to be at a slight tilt, a slight angle, or moved around a little."

The world can appear, according to Blue, askew, the way it does when you push in on the outer corners of your eyes with your fingers.

During one of the target studies, Blue was supposed to extend into one of the laboratories at the Psychical Research Foundation where a still-life had been set up: an oboe laid on a case, a bottle, and two frisbees. Blue described perceiving a black rectangular object with a tube coming out, a fair characterization of the oboe on the case. He also identified—explicitly—the bottle and the frisbees.

"I felt as though I were actually standing in the room, looking at the oboe," said Blue. "It's not the same feeling that I get when I have ESP perception, which is more like someone whispering the information to me inside my head when I'm definitely in my body. When I saw the oboe, it was just like I was in that room, even though my body was somewhere else in another building."

The detection experiments at first promised to be as ambiguous as the psychophysiological measurements and the response-to-target tests had been.

"We used a gerbil and a hamster for a while," said Morris. "They were tied into the polygraph in the target room, and we monitored any significant change in their activity which might indicate a reaction to Blue's out-of-the-body presence. We wouldn't know specifically when he would try to extend into the target room to make sure we wouldn't influence the behavior of the animals and to make sure we wouldn't place false interpretations on whatever data we collected. All we would know was that during a forty-minute period, Blue would attempt to visit us twice, and each visit would last approximately two minutes. Our clocks were synchronized so we could compare notes after the experiment was over.

"But the gerbil and the hamster didn't react in any significant way. We tried a snake, and the snake did sort of gnaw on the cage and got pretty upset at the time Blue was trying to visit it. It hyperventilated. There was definitely a reaction, but when we tried it again nothing happened."

Morris asked Blue to visit a thermistor, a heat detector, in his out-of-the-body state—which Blue claimed to do. But the thermistor registered no reaction. Morris asked Blue to dive in his out-of-the-body state through a large coil, in an experiment designed to see if Blue could change an electromagnetic field. No change. Morris used a photomultiplier to see if Blue could affect energy at some point in the electromagnetic spectrum, but that experiment offered up no significant results either.

"Then we tried another angle. We borrowed a spectrum analyzer from the electrical engineering department at Duke, a $10,000 piece of equipment that enables you to look along a wide range of the electromagnetic spectrum. You dial in the frequencies you want and check out what's happening on an oscilloscope in front of you. There's a green line along the bottom of the screen; and, for example, you can set the device to a certain wave length where the police calls are. Suddenly, there'll be a burst, a flare, that will hold for a while and then drop down. That will be the call.

"We tried it on two *oobies.* And the first time we got beautiful results. The burst corresponded to Blue's *oo-*

bie almost exactly. His *oobie* was two minutes long and so was the burst. There was perhaps a five-second lag on either end of the experience. Very interesting results. Especially since this occurred at 145 megahertz, which was a frequency that turned up in a poltergeist case in New York. The trouble is that on the second *oobie* we got essentially no results. We intend to explore this further once we can get access to the equipment again."

"During these tests," said Blue, "I'd feel as though I were really passing through a coil or, if there was a hoop, swinging on the hoop. It was as though I were actually in the room trying to influence the gadgets."

"In all these experiments," said Morris, "we were searching blindly. We had no idea what would work and what wouldn't. We were looking for something that could give us a handle on the experience."

Blue had been living at the Psychical Research Foundation so that when he went to the laboratory on the Duke University campus to leave his body and extend back to the target room, he would have the feeling of going home—an emotional nudge which Morris thought might make the out-of-the-body experiences more successful. Since the house where Blue was staying had the un-lived-in, vaguely abandoned feeling of a body recently vacated, Morris brought Blue two kittens to keep him company. Morris also wondered if a relationship between a human and an animal might positively affect the results of the detection studies.

Blue called the kittens Spirit and Soul, appropriate names for the scientific equivalents of familiars. Both were gray mottled, and Spirit had on its back a white Rorschach which Morris described as looking like the outline of a man—a good omen—but which could also be interpreted as a planarian, a flatworm with a triangular head.

In the late spring of 1973 when the kittens were about two-and-a-half months old, they were drafted to serve in the experiments. Each cat, first one and then the other, was placed in an enclosure thirty by eighty inches with thirty-inch-high walls and a base that was marked off into twenty-four squares; and Blue claimed that, like Alice straying through the looking glass into a world with a chessboard floor, he visited his pets.

The monitor in the target room could keep a record of each cat's activity by noting down the number of the squares the kittens visited within a certain period of time. If the animal ran from square 24 to square 1, the observer would jot 24—1. None of those in the target room knew exactly when Blue would attempt to visit the kitten, so they were unable to influence the animal's behavior.

During the first experiment, both kittens raced around the cage in patternless frightened loops; but when Morris tried the experiment a few days later, although Soul still rushed back and forth, Spirit abruptly became totally quiet during the time Blue, in his out-of-the-body state, was trying to visit and calm the animal.

"We did a four-night study, using that one cat," said Morris, "with the specific hypothesis that there would be a calming whenever Blue was extending into the target cage. We found that this indeed worked, and it worked every time.

"When we compared the maeows and squares crossed per minute during the non-*oobie* periods to the maeows and squares crossed per minute during the *oobie* periods, we found there was a mathematically meaningful difference.

"We didn't want to run the test too often because we didn't want to habituate the animal to the experience of being in the box, so the mathematical significance is not super skyrocketed, but it is definitely, dramatically beyond the acceptable levels of chance."

"I'd go into the box when I was out of the body and try to quiet the cat," said Blue. "Or I'd play with it, doing the same sort of things you might expect to do if you were in the body—tickle it behind the ears, pat it. And I'd be aware of the cat's response."

During the control periods, the kitten continually ran around the cage and maeowed thirty-seven times. During the time Blue had the sensations of being out of his body, visiting the kitten, the animal stopped running around the cage, did not maeow once, and seemed to be attentive to a presence in the enclosure that no human in the room could perceive.

The results, although limited, seem significant; and while the experiments with the cat do not prove Blue's ability to leave his body and extend some part of his self into another building, they do offer evidence that his out-of-the-body claims may have some basis in reality.

CHAPTER 9

At The Edge Of The Real

DURING THE TARGET STUDIES at the Psychical Research Foundation, Blue and Morris were joined by a young psychical researcher from California, D. Scott Rogo, a wary student of the paranormal, who came away from the experiments convinced that Blue possessed some extraordinary abilities. Rogo had been interested in out-of-the-body experiences since 1965, when he was fifteen years old. In junior high school he had pored over books on the occult and witchcraft; but, unsatisfied, he gradually turned to more scientific accounts of the unknown, books on parapsychology. While reading about a study of the medium Mrs. Keeler, which was carried out in the early 1900s by Prescott Hall, a Boston lawyer, Rogo ran across a diet that Mrs. Keeler claimed could induce out-of-the-body episodes. No nuts, lots of liquid, especially fruit juices; meat in moderation.

Two weeks after starting the diet, he came home, lay down on the bed in his room, and had just begun to fall asleep when he felt his body become cataleptic. He tried closing his eyes, and abruptly he was standing next to his rigid body, looking down at it. When he tried to leave the room, he woke up in his body.

Not long after this first experience, on a hot afternoon during the summer of 1965, he was on the bed when his body was seized by a pulsing sensation, the way a thumb feels after being accidentally smashed with a hammer. Kneeling on the bed, facing the headboard, he gazed at his body. This time he succeeded in leaving his room. In the hallway his two dogs started barking at him; in the living room he saw a relative sitting on the couch and reading a book. The phone rang—a modern equivalent to the Gothic church bell tolling wandering spirits back to their shells—and Rogo found himself lying on his bed in his room. The dogs, the reading relative, the telephone ring—meager evidence—all checked out.

His third experience occurred in October, 1965. He woke in the middle of the night with the uneasy feeling that he had been out of his body. As he was trying to reorient himself, he felt catapulted from his flesh; and when he glanced down from where he was floating, he saw a third self hovering between him and his physical body. Me, myself, and I—a trinity usually invoked for emphasis, not description.

Just when he was getting used to popping in and out of his body with the ease of a waiter passing back and forth through a swinging door, the experiences stopped; he no longer was able to fully leave his body. However, for the next year he continued to have partial separations.

One night in 1967 he awoke aware of the dual consciousness that he'd come to recognize as a sign of the out-of-the-body experience. But when he tried to separate from his physical self, he got stuck, his out-of-the-body body sitting, his material body lying down. He couldn't free his legs and feet—it was as if they were trapped under layers of heavy quilts. The next morning when he climbed from bed, he almost doubled over from the excruciating pain he felt cinched around his waist. Shortly after that even the partial experiences stopped.

He continued to read about the phenomenon while he was an undergraduate at the University of Cincinnati in Ohio, and at California State University at Northridge. By the time he received his B.A. in 1971, he had written two books on paranormal phenomena.

Rogo has a flair for the quietly dramatic—walking on broken glass to prove there is nothing unusual about the fakirs' trick, indulging in unpretentious showmanship to deflate myth and mystics with the same nonchalance certain psychics display in trying to create mystery.

"A lot of psychics, quite frankly, are liars," he said. "I wouldn't trust most of them, particularly a few that have been traipsing around the country lately. But Blue is one of the most one hundred per cent honest on-the-level, guys I've ever met. He is totally convincing, even if you don't believe. You don't believe?" he added.

Rogo talked like an early Christian, questioning a cynical but sympathetic Roman.

"He's open, he's reliable, and he is an excellent psychology student. He knows what standards of evidence are, and he knows what responsible scientific behavior is. While I was at Durham, I got to know him well. He was living in the meditation center, a small building behind the main lab. I'd spend all day with him. I'd take my meals with him. I'd watch TV at night with him, goof around with him, stay up late talking with him, go to movies with him. I was with the guy just about every waking moment. After that much contact, you get a feel for a person.

"But I still wouldn't believe in the reality of his experiences unless I had participated in some of the experiments. When Blue visited the snake in his out-of-the-body state, it stopped its typical maneuvering around the cage and started literally to attack. It sort of bit at the air, viciously, for about twenty seconds. Twenty seconds which were right in the middle of the time Blue, without knowing what was going on in the laboratory, claimed to be out of his body and in the cage with the snake."

Despite the discrepancies in the two accounts of what occurred during the test with the snake—Morris saying it "did sort of gnaw on the cage"; Rogo saying it "sort of bit at the air"—it seems that the snake did exhibit a radical change in its behavior when Blue felt that he had entered the cage in his out-of-the-body state. But the discrepancies do illuminate the difficulty in depending too heavily on personal observation when there is great leeway for interpretation.

Similar problems shadow the reports of the people who were used as human detectors and who claimed to see flashing lights and glowing orbs when Blue was trying to extend into their presence.

"When I'm out of my body and I feel like my consciousness is just a ball of light, everything seems to flicker," said Blue. "I feel as though I flicker through things."

One night at the end of the summer Rogo woke after three hours of sleep and saw, out of the corner of his eye, a glowing red sphere about the size of a baseball darting past the bed. He made a note of the time: 3:22 A.M.

"The next day I saw Blue," said Rogo, "but he didn't say anything. I asked him if he had tried to appear to me the night before. He said, yes, he had. I asked him what time it was when he tried. He said between three and three-thirty."

Blue was unable to define what kind of a presence he thought he was when in the out-of-the-body state. He could only define how he felt.

"Sometimes your body is just lying there, quietly vibrating, and you just roll out and get up and walk away, as calmly as if you were getting out of bed. You feel as if your physical body's still lying there and something else has gotten up—something lighter.

"There are other times when it all happens very fast, rushing like an express train, and it looks like you're going to hit the wall across the room."

He described what happened in the out-of-the-body state as if it were as real as what he experienced while in his body, but at the same time he leached the reality from the events by reducing his out-of-the-body world to a solipsism. It doesn't feel like anything to pass through a wall, he explained, because "It's only a thought. When you're out of your body, you think things into existence. Things may be real without being real in the way we usually use the word.

"Normally people go along in our everyday reality, the reality they share with others, the reality everybody agrees on; but beyond that consensus, each individual exists in his own reality. It's very difficult to explain because our society is so used to describing things in terms of real and unreal, rather than real and . . . real."

According to Blue, the solipsistic reality in which the out-of-the-body experience occurred interacted somehow with our everyday reality, the implication being that whatever connected the out-of-the-body state with the physical body also joined the idiosyncratic and everyday realities.

"Once, when I was out of my body," he said, trying to clarify this sense of inhabiting many equally valid realities, "I passed through this dark area and suddenly came to a lighted area—a room. I had been to that room before. It was familiar, one of the rooms where I had classes. I saw myself standing in that room, but I was like a black silhouette, and the silhouette of my body was also like a window. When I looked into that window, through me, I could see everything that was going on, hear people talking. Then I came out of that silhouette, and went back into my physical body.

"A week later I went into a room, the same room where I had seen that silhouette, for a class. And we were all sitting around this fireplace. The farthest thing from my mind was that *oobie*.

"Along about a certain time in the class I started getting this very strange feeling—very, very drowsy. All of a sudden I fell back, and I was awake, but I was not awake in a normal way, not really awake in the class, although I was still aware of the class.

"I had this sensation that I was behind myself, looking through me. Everything that was going on was what I had seen the week before when I had been out of my body and looking through that silhouette of myself into that room."

Blue's cosmology was not fully elaborated, but he suggested that the solipsistic reality not only interpenetrates with everyday reality but, in fact, everyday reality may only be a useful set of myths which we all agreed upon little by little as we were growing up. Once we are adults, we forget that reality is only a fiction which we invented. We become like Morris's first few subjects who created rules—they could get out of their body, but not out of the room—and then slavishly followed them.

If reality is furnished by our imagination, then, by this logic, we could each dismantle the universe by imaginatively annihilating everything that exists until all that was left would be our consciousness. This un-creation is a reversal of the cosmogonic myth in the *Brihadaranyaka Upanishad,* a Hindu text over two thousand years old, according to which the Universal Consciousness flickered into being like a fluorescent light coming on in a dark room; and at that point,

> . . . the universe was nothing but the Self in the form of a man. It looked around and saw that there was nothing but itself, whereupon its first shout was, "It is I!" . . . However, he still lacked delight. . . . He was exactly as large as a man and a woman embracing. This Self then divided itself in two parts. . . .

The All, now two, confronted itself, perceiving the world from separate egos, an experience that conforms to the definition of an out-of-the-body episode.

This similarity between the out-of-the-body phenomenon and the Hindu myth may indicate that the out-of-the-body experience is an archetypal event, a replaying on a smaller stage of an occurrence which was—depending on one's metaphysical bias—either historically or psychically true. Or the perceived similarity may be the result of the influence of Eastern philosophy in shaping Western assumptions about a phenomenon which could or could not be paranormal.

If the out-of-the-body experience is, in fact, paranormal and not merely the eruption of an archetypal event or the cross-cultural assimilation of a myth, there was nothing in the results of the experiments with Blue to conclusively prove that the apparently paranormal event that took place was an example of consciousness actually separating from the body and not some form of ESP or psychokinesis. And Blue made only a subjective distinction between the out-of-the-body experience and ESP and psychokinesis. If he felt he was out of his body when there was evidence that ESP or psychokinetic phenomena had occurred, he assumed the episode was an out-of-the-body experience. Morris accepted Blue's felt distinction as a basis for labeling what Blue did in the laboratory out-of-the-body. This was a significant flaw in his otherwise reasonable experimental strategy of staking out all the locations—psychophysiological measurements, responses to targets, detection studies—where the out-of-the-body consciousness might manifest itself. He depended too much on Blue's feelings of being separated from his flesh for his definition of the experience and did not allow for an experimental distinction between ESP, PK, and out-of-the-body functioning.

The assumption which underlay the experiments was that if the subject claimed he felt out of his body at the same time that certain evidential phenomena occurred, then the sensations of being out of the body could be linked by the coincidence in time to the other phenomena. The problem with this assumption was that it rested upon the acceptance of an undefined bridge between the subject's feelings and the evidential phenomena. This connection, between Blue's sensations and, for example, the kitten's actions, is precisely what the experiment must try to discover. It cannot be assumed.

The results of Morris's work, while certainly supporting the possibility that something paranormal had happened, did not define what that something was; and that something was not necessarily what Blue felt it was. The distinctions among the various types of paranormal phenomena which Morris had failed to draw were, however, being made in the out-of-the-body experiments at the American Society for Psychical Research.

CHAPTER 10

ASPR

THE AMERICAN SOCIETY FOR PSYCHICAL RESEARCH—
like a respectable old-fashioned eccentric matron, all
bombazine and lace with a handkerchief tucked in at
the wrist—occupies a townhouse on Seventy-third
Street off Central Park West in New York City. In 1884
Sir William Fletcher Barrett, one of the principal
founders of the British Society for Psychical Research,
instigated a number of American intellectuals, especially from Boston and Cambridge, Massachusetts, to
create a sister institution to the British society in the
United States; and by January, 1885, the ASPR was established.

When Blue Harary first visited the society in December, 1971, the out-of-the-body-experience studies were
just being launched under the guidance of Dr. Karlis
Osis, who had been made the society's research director in 1962.

"When I started in parapsychology," said Osis, "I would not have done a project like this. Out-of-the-body phenomena was a bit too far out."

Osis, his face wrinkled like a partially deflated balloon, spoke in a soft singsong that tended to drop to a conspiratorial level when he wanted to make a point. In conversation his attention wandered like a spirit absently searching for its body, touching one subject briefly, floating off to another subject—jumps that were not quite non sequiturs if you searched for the ghostly cable connecting the two randomly related ideas. His accent was thick, creating wonderful misapprehended Thurberesque flashes: "Inductive years" became "doctor's ears"; "life after death" became "lilac bursts."

He was born on a farm in Riga, Latvia, the day after Christmas, 1917. His father, a strict rationalist, did not believe in any superstitions, ancient or modern; there was no talk in the family about paranormal phenomena.

As a child Osis contracted tuberculosis and was bedridden at the same time an old aunt who had suffered a stroke lay dying at the other end of their farmhouse. One day Osis, a feverish fifteen, lay resting when he suddenly saw his room come alive with light.

"Not a light you could read a paper by," he said, "but that's the best way to describe it. The light was in me too. I'd never experienced anything like it. I was amazed and filled with great joy. I couldn't understand why I was so happy. The joy had a quality I'd never felt before. And then somebody walked into the room and said, 'Auntie just died.' "

Osis's joy at his aunt's death was not a cruel pleasure. He wasn't happy that she had died, he was happy with her, as he experienced, perhaps telepathically, the elation which often precedes death. This experience understandably fascinated him; and the fascination stayed with him as he grew older as nostalgia and goal, like two facing mirrors, reflecting the present in the past and in the future.

He received his Ph.D. in psychology in 1950 from the University of Munich in Germany; and in 1957, after working as a research associate of Dr. Rhine's at the Parapsychology Laboratory at Duke University, Osis was made research director of the Parapsychology Foundation in New York City. While there, he indulged his curiosity in death raptures by studying the experiences people have at the moment of dying. The Parapsychology Foundation published his findings in 1961 as a booklet, "Deathbed Observations by Physicians and Nurses."

"I sent out 10,000 questionnaires," said Osis, "and I received 640 back. According to those doctors and nurses who answered, one out of twenty patients seemed to experience an elevated mood just before death. Also, there were 884 cases in which the dying patient saw hallucinations with non-human content. Visions of heaven or hell or apparitions of dead relatives. This I found very curious. But some people believe in Santa Claus; I don't. I thought, *Maybe we can think about this in a different way.* I began to think about out-of-body experiences."

In 1971 Osis advertised for out-of-the-body adepts, and he received one hundred responses. Those who lived near New York City were tested, like Blue, in the society's headquarters. Those who lived outside of New York City were invited to fly in to Osis's office and identify targets arranged on his coffee table.

"This is one of the targets we used," Osis said, gesturing at an arrangement of triple-colored stripes (red, white, and black—colors of the flag of Upper Volta; "No meaning to the choice," said Osis). The stripes formed a *V* in front of a small sphinx-like figurine. From one direction, the figurine looked like a woman's face; from the opposite direction, it looked like an easy chair. The pedestal of the sphinx was an old UNICEF Christmas card box.

If the out-of-the-body experience is real, Osis explained, "we wanted to see if someone could visit us in that out-of-body state and position himself in relation to the target. That way we could see if his consciousness was organized from a single point of view or from no particular point of view.

"If he looked at the target from this direction, he would see the chair. If he looked at the target from the other side, he would see the smiling Venus face. If he looked at it from above, he would see a square blob. Or would he see it all at the same time: the chair, the face, everything? This is important.

"In an out-of-body experience people seem to perceive from one specific point of view. ESP usually lacks a spatial organization. By using a target which looks different from different directions, we can see if there is a difference between ESP and out-of-body states, or if out-of-body states are simply terrific bursts of ESP, combined with fantasies of flying.

"When we did this first experiment, we were looking for someone who could control the out-of-body experience; and we found three people who were promising."

One of Osis's subjects, Claudette Kiely, lived in an area of Massachusetts that had served as a model for the landscapes in the horror tales of H. P. Lovecraft. She had grown up in Keene, New Hampshire, in a house

bordering a cemetery. As a child, whenever she became frightened of night-shadows, she would fix her
attention on a picture of an angel guiding two children
across a bridge, which her mother had cut off a calendar
and tacked to the wall. In parochial school she was
spellbound by tales of saints who could levitate and
bilocate, but she was told that paranormal experiences
were signs of divinity in man and they never occurred
to average people.

When she was sixteen, however, she had a precognitive dream.

"A friend of mine had just gotten her driver's li-
cense," Kiely said, "and her grandfather had given her
his new Pontiac so we could go to a high school basketball tournament in Portsmouth, ninety miles away. This
was in the early fifties, and we were very strictly controlled, so this was a big adventure for us.

"I had a dream about this trip. We were driving
through Hillsboro on the way home, and my friend
said she wanted a cup of coffee because she was getting sleepy. Diagonally across the street to the left,
we saw a place that had a light on. It looked like a
drugstore which would probably have a counter.
There was a dark car parked in front, and we pulled
up next to it.

"We entered the store. There was a gentleman sitting on a stool at the counter, wearing a London Fog-
type raincoat and a soft felt hat. He looked at us and
said, 'What on earth are you girls doing out at this time
of night?' We told him. And he said, 'Well, for God-
sakes, be careful going home that no one tries to road-
block you on Concord Hill.' He indicated someone was
going to try to harm us in some way."

She ignored the dream, assuming it was due to the

excitement of going off on a long trip for the first time without her parents. But on the way home from the basketball tournament, on the outskirts of Hillsboro, her friend sleepily said she wanted a cup of coffee; and, slowing down, she added, "Look, there's a light over there. Maybe they have a coffee counter."

Across the road was the drugstore from Kiely's dream. And the dark-colored car.

"Oh, my God, don't stop," said Kiely. "Keep going. Just don't stop."

Her friend didn't stop. By the time Kiely had finished describing her dream, they were approaching Concord Hill, where the road snaked through a deserted, rocky area outside of Keene. As they came around a bend, a car that was parked on the shoulder of the road snapped on its lights and started pulling out in front of them to force them to stop. Kiely's friend floored the accelerator, and they swerved around the car, escaping whatever horror either fancy or fate had teased them with.

"After that experience," she said, "other things began happening. ESP, things like that. And sometimes I would get the feeling that I was out of my body."

Kiely was an occultist, looking to the paranormal for the satisfactions of religion, not science. Her conversation was littered with the ghostly terms of spiritualism, words with meanings that dissolve into air and vanish when you try to define them. She read Sri Paul Twitchell—leader of a West Coast cult called Eckankar, whose members claim they commute regularly in their astral bodies between Earth and Venus—with the same seriousness as she read C. G. Jung. Reincarnation, possession, magnetic attractions. . . . Her world was a grab-bag of the strange and the quaint.

And I was pleased by her odd mix of beliefs, which argued against accepting her (and perhaps any) paranormal explanation of out-of-the-body experiences. The experiments with Blue Harary at the Psychical Research Foundation had been convincing, and I wanted unconvincing evidence as a counterbalance. I welcomed her unusual behavior (she meditated while listening to Jim Nabors and Elvis Presley ballads) as *ad hominem* proof that her out-of-the-body experiences were imaginary. If Osis thought her convincing, then, since I was more ready to disbelieve than believe, that would make me distrust Osis.

The flaw, of course, was that Osis discounted her interpretation of the out-of-the-body experience—that it was a religious event, a god-given "reward for hungering after spiritual good"—and looked only at the evidence. What she believed was not as important as what she could experimentally do. And although the evidence was weak, she did seem to be able to do something.

Kiely had answered Osis's advertisement, and late in 1972 the American Society for Psychical Research contacted her to arrange for a series of experiments. Osis asked her to attempt to visit his office (which she had never seen) in the out-of-body state at certain agreed-upon times.

The first experiment took place on December 13, 1972. At ten o'clock in the evening Kiely asked her children to be quiet. She put on a loose gown, prayed for the protection of the people to whom she was trying to project, lay down on the bed, and started to relax her body from the toes up, while breathing deeply. When she was completely relaxed, she imagined her body was rolling itself up toward her head. She felt a physical heaviness in her chest, a sensation of expanding.

"Usually I go out through the top of my head," she said. "Sometimes I'll hear a high-pitched squeal, or a rumble, or a crack. And then I'll be somewhere else."

She found herself in a variety store in New York City. The owner was closing, but he had just allowed a man and a woman in.

"I'll put some water on for coffee," he told them.

Kiely noticed the woman's shoes, spring shoes that were soaked from walking through slush, and the woman's legs, which were spattered with mud.

"I lost the sound track while I was watching her shoes," said Kiely, describing the experience as though it had been a movie. "And then I realized I was supposed to be at the ASPR."

The grocery store vanished, and she was looking at a tall bird and a small, elaborately carved natural-wood box, both of which she described in her report.

During that experiment Dr. Osis's coffee table was divided by a large piece of cardboard, and the target objects were arranged on the side of the cardboard nearest the fireplace.

"What Claudette Kiely saw corresponded to the objects on the side of the cardboard nearer the couch," said Bonnie Prescari, Dr. Osis's research associate. "She said she saw 'a tall glass bird, white and marbleized colors'—I'm reading from her file—and 'a carved box.' What, in fact, was there was a large papier-mâché parrot of different colors, which was sculpted to make it look like it had feathers, and a watering can standing on a box. But this information, to the extent that it was accurate, could have been picked up through clairvoyance as well as through an out-of-the-body experience."

All that could be safely concluded was that Kiely had feelings of being out of her body at the same time she gave some evidence of non-sensory perception.

The results of the second and third experiments, which were done on January 5 and 11, were also mixed, possible indications of out-of-the-body experiences confused with what seemed more like clairvoyance. The fourth and fifth experiments, January 30 and February 6, were failures, and Osis turned his attention to other subjects and other experiments.

CHAPTER 11

OOBE, ESP, or PK?

WHILE WORKING ON EXPERIMENTS designed to make distinctions among the out-of-the-body experience, ESP, and PK, Osis began using as a subject a New York City artist named Ingo Swann who seemed to have a wide range of paranormal powers. In 1972 Swann had participated in a study at City College of New York run by Dr. Gertrude R. Schmeidler, who found evidence that Swann could change the temperature of an object placed at a distance from him in a way that suggested authentic psychokinetic phenomena.

Swann sat about three feet in front of a Dynograph which was used to record the temperatures of four thermistors that had been taped to pieces of either bakelite or graphite to facilitate his possible PK. Each thermistor recorded independently of the others, and all were extremely sensitive. All four were sealed within Thermos bottles so that there would be little likelihood of their being affected by any force other than Swann's apparent paranormal abilities.

Although Dr. Schmeidler admitted that the temperature changes were not dramatic, she claimed they were meaningful. She reported on the results of her tests in an article which was published in the October, 1973, issue of *The Journal of the American Society for Psychical Research*, "PK Effects Upon Continuously Recorded Temperature":

> Seven of Ingo's ten scores are statistically significant, and five are highly significant. . . . Each of the significant differences is in the direction specified by instructions; that is, the recordings show more change toward hotter temperature in the test periods with "Make it hotter" instructions than in the test periods with "Make it colder" instructions.

Ingo seemed to be able to change the temperature of a test object more than one degree during one of the forty-five second test periods, and Dr. Schmeidler concluded that there was evidence which strongly suggested that "Ingo could change recorded temperature by PK."

Ostensible proof of PK, however, does not guarantee that the subject can necessarily separate his consciousness from his body, although susceptibility to one paranormal power seems to ensure susceptibility to others. In his out-of-the-body experiments with Osis at the ASPR, Swann gave evidence that he could exteriorize his consciousness as easily as he could affect the temperature of a piece of bakelite sealed in a Thermos bottle.

Osis and his associates had designed an experiment which emphasized the nature of out-of-the-body perception even more than the Venus-face—easy-chair test had. The subject would sit in a dimly lit room, wired to a polygraph in another room which recorded his psychophysiological changes. He would try to extend his consciousness to targets which had been placed on a shelf that was suspended two feet from the ceiling of the laboratory. On each side of a partition, which divided the shelf, were trays containing objects arranged to look different from opposite directions.

In "New ASPR Research on Out-of-the-Body Experiences," a short report Osis wrote for the Summer, 1972, issue of the *American Society for Psychical Research Newsletter*, Osis said:

> We used objects having strong form and color, e.g., an umbrella, a black leather scissor-case, an apple. . . . The results were evaluated by blind judging: that is, a psychologist was asked to match up . . . responses without knowing which target they were meant for.

Swann, sketching what he saw on each side of the partition, achieved a perfect score: eight tries out of eight. The odds against this happening by chance are approximately 40,000 to 1. During the experiments his heart rate, breathing, and blood flow appeared normal, but his brain waves seemed to accelerate.

"I'd say fewer alpha waves and more beta waves," said Osis. "We found the voltage seemed to decrease when Ingo said he was out."

Swann's perception also seemed to be definitely organized from a single point of view, which indicated that if he were receiving information through paranormal faculties, then what was at work was probably out-of-the-body functioning, not ESP.

Swann, however, doesn't like to admit he has any paranormal abilities.

"Frankly, you would have to say that I don't claim to have out-of-the-body experiences," Swann said. "And I hope you would make that quite clear. That's where the trouble comes from: some guy walks out and says, 'Ah ha, I'm this or I'm that,' and everybody wants to prove that's not the case at all."

But Swann's denial, like Caesar's rejection of the crown, was a coy, politic way of accepting what he seemed to put off. His disclaimer was a semantic dodge. He preferred the term *exteriorization* to the phrase *out-of-the-body experience,* and although he quibbled about the concept, he admitted that he believed consciousness could separate from the physical body.

"People have experiences which can be called out-of-the-body," he said, "but since we don't know where consciousness sits in relationship to the body, it doesn't mean very much to call it that. It would be better to say the body is out of them; they have moved their center of organized awareness, and the body has become part of the environment which they perceive. The implication is that there is an element of human consciousness that is not in any way dependent upon the body."

Swann, who lived in a loft on the Bowery, talked in a drawl that was half-Southwestern United States and half-East Village *Weltschmerz,* an ironic accent which served to distance him from passionate involvement in what he was describing at the moment. He tried to present information about his paranormal experiences devoid of bias, as though he had been only a witness to the events, not the participant.

"I hope you'll excuse the mess," he said, waving at a

floor cluttered with dumped books. "My bookcase exploded this morning. I've had some breakthroughs in psychokinesis recently, and things like this have been happening."

He picked up a Vicks inhaler from the table and used it first in one nostril, then in the other, snorting elegantly as though it were snuff or cocaine.

"An heirloom from my grandmother was broken in the explosion."

The loft was divided by a curtain as though it were a theater. On the walls were Swann's paintings, large canvases of star-fields, which looked more like backgrounds for *Tom Corbett and His Space Cadets* than authentic visions of galaxies.

"Any artist derives his subject matter from personal data," said Swann. "I got involved in the possibilities of using extraterrestrial situations as concepts. I could say that one day I was just traveling around when I had nothing else to do and I found myself looking at the constellation of Sagittarius from a point several million miles outside of the earth's frame of reference, and I reproduced it in a painting. But that just excites people."

Swann was born on September 14, 1933, in Telluride, Colorado, as Ingo Swan. He added the second *n* after a numerologist told him the extra letter would bring him wealth. When he was three years old, he had the sensation of separating from his body during a tonsil operation and watching the doctor slice at his throat. When he was a little older, he claimed he used to leave his body to swoop through the Rocky Mountains, following the veins of metal in the stone.

He studied biology at Westminster College in Salt Lake City, Utah, but he became an apostate when he argued with his monitor about the theory of evolution.

"I said, 'The theory of evolution is really just a theory. It's not a fact at all.' And my monitor said, 'No, it's not a theory. It's a fact.' I was pleased last year when the school system in Los Angeles finally understood that evolution is only a theory, it's not proven, and they had their textbooks altered to indicate that." Swann took pride in being an independent thinker.

He received his undergraduate degree in art and biology in 1955, and after three years in the Army, moved to New York City to paint. Despite his childhood paranormal experiences, he did not seriously explore psychic phenomena and the occult until 1959, when his curiosity was pricked by a change in the style of his painting.

"After all," he said, "if you suddenly feel inspired to paint astrological symbols, then you try to find out what implication this has."

To discover what may have caused the occult subjects to slip from his brush, he browsed through Jungian psychology and, unsatisfied, plunged into more esoteric studies.

"As a side issue I began to read about psychical research," he said, "and it never dawned on me that I would ever become a participant in experiments. But one of the things that changed my mind about that was a chinchilla I bought as a house pet.

"This was a unique animal; this animal was telepathic. It could understand what was being thought by anybody around it, especially if the thought occurred in anybody's head to put him in his cage. He had a definite and reproduceable reaction.

"This started me thinking: if a chinchilla can do it, why can't a man?"

Although Swann insists that his interest in the paranormal reflects a scientific bias, unsullied by *popular* (he said the word as though he were chewing a spoiled fig) credulity or faddishness, his speculations about his chinchilla sounded more like stoned-out parlor games than controlled research. And from 1969 to 1971 he dallied with Scientology, a craze which is equal parts religion, debased psychoanaylsis, and science fiction.

Faddist or not, Swann seemed to be able to exercise paranormal abilities in a controlled, reproducible form. Osis once referred to him as "our star subject." Janet Mitchell, who had worked with Osis on the out-of-the-body experiments, said that "Ingo has the best developed abilities of anyone I've ever seen, and I've been working in the field for seven years." But after working with Osis and his associates for nearly a year, Swann left the ASPR experiments; and Osis began concentrating on studies using a Maine psychic, Alex Tanous, as a subject.

Tanous, quietly mysterious, with hypnotic eyes, looked like an MGM mystic. Part of his magnetism was an appeal to vanity. He gazed at you with rapt attention, all the furrows in his brow tending down to a point above the bridge of his nose as though they were caused by a pulled drawstring.

He worked a subtle flattery on strangers, saying, "Well, we must have a psychic bond. When I saw you across the room, I knew that was you. I'm sure you have powers too," playing on everyone's desire to feel special, to feel that they too have extraordinary abilities.

He was born in 1926 in Van Buren, Maine, a small town on the New Brunswick border.

"Both of my parents were psychic," he said, "and

they started working with me when I was eighteen months old, teaching me how to use my psychic abilities."

He first experienced the sensation of leaving his body when he was five years old. His consciousness seemed to become a mass of mobile intelligent energy. But apart from his psychic episodes—which he spoke about too readily—he was guarded about his childhood, smiling away the Depression, when he had to pick potatoes to help support his family, shrugging off his high school years.

"I was under the impression everyone could do these things," he said. "I was surprised when I found out that wasn't true."

He went to Boston College in Massachusetts, receiving a B.A. in history in 1958 and an M.A. in philosophy in 1961.

"According to his record, he was a special student," said an official at the Boston College alumni office. "Someone also scribbled down here, 'ESP nut.'"

In 1964 he received his M.A. in theology from Fordham University in New York, and four years later he began performing as a psychic, engaging in vaudevillian razzle-dazzle. An article in the Friday, August 27, 1971, issue of the Utica, New York, *Observer-Dispatch* reported:

> . . . Tanous . . . was able to solidify . . . a small ball of light that was evident to this reporter. . . . A 500-watt bulb is flashed on and off, eight to ten times, only inches away from his eyes. The room is in total darkness.
>
> He then stares intently into his outstretched arms and shapes a form of a ball with his hands. Within seconds, a bluish, misty ball of light appears there.
>
> Many in the crowd could not see the light. . . . But

there were those who claimed they saw it and they were adamant in their belief. They were backed up by the fact that at least a dozen Polaroid pictures, taken of . . . Tanous in total darkness, showed the round ball of light.

Tanous claimed to have predicted Lyndon Johnson's decision not to seek reelection in 1968, Judy Garland's death in 1969, Charles DeGaulle's death in 1970, George McGovern's nomination as the Democratic Party's candidate for the Presidency in 1971, and Harry Truman's death in 1972. Although his predictions were often vague enough to admit many interpretations ("There will be earthquakes in Europe" in 1968; "The kidnapping of an American official will make headlines" in 1972), he was convincing enough for Herman Boudreau, chief of the Freeport, Maine, police department, to contact him to help locate an eight-year-old boy who had vanished on June 13, 1972.

Boudreau led Tanous through the apartment house in which the boy lived and drove him around the neighborhood. Tanous announced that the boy was dead and the body was wrapped and hidden somewhere in the house, which turned out to be true; the boy's corpse was found in the apartment house, rolled in a blanket and tucked under the bed of a thirty-three-year old shoe factory worker (whom Tanous had sketched).

Tanous had had enough psychic successes to suggest his claims may be true, and yet like many psychics he seemed to mix fact and fancy freely.

He had seven younger brothers, all of whom, Tanous insisted, possessed psychic powers, which they used in their work. But one brother, Tom Tanous, a high school history teacher in Beverly, Massachusetts, shied from admitting it. "I was just elected president of the Massachusetts Teachers' Association," he said. "I can't make a statement."

Another, Wakine Tanous, a Maine state senator who was running for the Republican nomination for governor at the time, would not make himself available for comment; and a third, Charles Tanous, who was managing Wakine's campaign, denied he'd ever had psychic experiences.

Tanous also improved reality in a lecture flier in which he claimed to have received a Ph.D. in philosophy from Fordham University, a degree the registrar at Fordham had no record of and which Tanous later admitted he did not get.

"There's a narrow line separating the psychic and the paranoiac," Tanous himself said. And psychics, like paranoiacs, are inclined to fill in gaps and make connections among orderless events like a child joining with chalk the random pockmarks on a sidewalk. Stonehenge becomes a landing base for flying saucers, creatures from outer space become aspects of God, and God becomes the source of psychic powers. Chaos is unacceptable; the world must make sense. The psychic's tendency to amend reality is, at base, the need of a rationalist. Blue Harary began to seem remarkable, not so much for his ability to leave his body, but for how much he resisted the temptation to elaborate on that experience.

"I'm aware that psychics do over-claim quite a bit," said Osis, when I asked him about Tanous's unsubstantiated statements that he had received a doctorate from Fordham, that his brothers had psychic powers, that he has seen UFOs. "They usually have artistic temperaments. In a way, we look for that. Rhine once said, 'If you have a subject who keeps every appointment, the experiment probably won't work.'

"So our position is this: we never do experiments which depend on the morals of a subject. It's the scores that come out in the controlled laboratory experiments which are important."

Since the earlier experiments with Ingo Swann indicated that out-of-the-body vision seemed to mimic physical sight, Osis decided to test in his experiments with Tanous whether or not out-of-the-body vision followed the laws of optics. He abandoned the shelf targets in favor of an illusion box.

"This is an apparatus which has a small opening that you look through," said Osis. "Inside is a two-mirror system which reflects the target so that when you look into the opening you see an illusion, not what the target really is. A small letter *d* might look like a *p*."

He invited me to look into the box, which I did. Inside, I saw an area divided into four quadrants of different colors. In one quadrant was a design of a snake.

"That is not as you see it," Osis said. "The snake is not where you think it is. Now, if our subject gives us a response describing what you see, this would indicate that he is perceiving from this point in space in front of the viewing window. If he had a general ESP X-ray of the box, he would see how things really are. The indications are that the subjects perceive from here, at the viewing window. We worked with Tanous, using the illusion box, and he did produce reasonably well. The scores indicated that the odds against his getting the targets right from chance were 100 to 1. With no man do we expect spectacular scores, but I think that suggests he does have the ability to do something paranormal. And it seems from the way he perceived the targets in the experiments that what he can do might be out-of-body."

According to Osis, Tanous's out-of-the-body consciousness appeared able to adjust to its environmental situation—in certain cases, for example, he had to move his point of view higher to peer into the window of the illusion box. This ability to interact with the world in a disembodied state would not be manifest if he were receiving information through ESP. Furthermore, if Tanous had been gaining knowledge of the targets in the illusion box through ESP, he would have described what was actually there. Because he described the illusion, which would have been apparent only when seen through the viewing window, the results of the tests added more evidence to what had already been gathered in the sessions with Ingo Swann. Not only did some paranormal experiences seem authentic, but—in certain cases of perceiving information at a distance—there did seem to be an out-of-the-body function which was distinct from ESP.

This seeming out-of-the-body function—or at least that part of it which is comparable to vision—operates, if the evidence is correct, similarly to in-body vision, although it does not seem to be as good as in-body vision.

"It is probably more like vision in the dark," said Osis. "You see some outlines, and you fill in. So your wishes creep in too, because you don't want to leave blanks. This is a problem. Also, sometimes our subjects run into what in psychology we call the figure-ground effect. They have problems separating what is the figure from what is the background. It is like—Have you seen the picture where, if you focus in one way, you see a vase and, if you focus in another way, you see instead the profiles of two women, defined by the contours of the vase? Like that. And that is a problem."

If the subject perceives an image formed from the background and not the target object—sees, for example, the profiles of two women and not the vase—then the scorer might record that session as a miss, not a hit. But the figure-ground effect, despite its problems, provides additional evidence that out-of-body perception is not ESP, since figure-ground confusion would only exist if the out-of-the-body information gathering were, at least partly, some form of disembodied vision.

The central question modulates from "How real is the out-of-the-body experience?" to "How is the out-of-the-body experience real?" How can such an unlikely phenomenon exist within our traditional conception of reality? How will we have to reshape our conception of reality to fit the evidence that the out-of-the-body phenomenon may be real and not merely a form of extrasensory perception?

CHAPTER 12

In The Suburbs
Of The Unknown

ONE OF THE FIRST SERIOUS PARAPSYCHOLOGISTS to suggest the need for revising our twentieth century conception of reality in order to explain phenonema like the out-of-the-body experience was Rosalind Heywood, one of the doyennes of British psychical research and the woman Arthur Koestler described as "catalyzer-in-chief" in the dedication to his book on parapsychology, *The Roots Of Coincidence.* She became interested in out-of-the-body experiences on a summer night in the early 1920s in a bedroom of a chateau in Anjou, France. She had decided to wake her husband so she could escape the oppressive silence by making love, but before she could rouse him, she realized abruptly she was two. One Rosalind Heywood squirmed on the mattress while another Rosalind Heywood quietly, contemptuously watched the first from the foot of the carved bedstead.

"Each of us had a body. The one in the bed was wearing pink, but the other one was wearing white. I have no idea why. Consciousness was present in both. At one minute the white me was at the bottom of the bed, and at another minute it had rejoined the pink me."

Rosalind Heywood, at the end of her seventh decade, sat on the couch in the living room of her family's house in Wimbledon, England, not far from the tennis courts where the international competitions are held—a house which looks as Edwardian as the Darlings' home in which Peter Pan temporarily lost his shadow. Her voice fluted up and down, following a conversational sine wave; and the only indication of her age was the occasional pause, the flash of inward focus, when something she said in the present flared, illuminating something she had done in the past.

"To ask if an out-of-the-body experience is real doesn't apply," Rosalind Heywood said. "We always try to explain odd experiences in terms of everyday time and space, and I don't think that makes sense. When I was a child, we were taught Euclidean geometry. Now, I understand, there are several other geometries. There's no use forcing those geometries into Euclidean geometry. They won't go. They're different in kind. We're so busy trying to define one set of circumstances in terms of another set of circumstances which may not apply that we knot ourselves up in our own questions."

She was released from the thrall of turn-of-the-century rationalism by the horrors of World War I. After the sack of Louvain, the appearance of poison gas at Ypres, and the carnage at Verdun, the only way to avoid believing man was evil was to believe he was in great measure irrational. And, like many English women of her generation and class who, during the war, had cracked through the old conventions which had restricted them to chattering in the parlor, once the war was over she started to exercise her intelligence by exploring the irrational in the form of psychic speculation—one of the few fields not monopolized by dominant husbands.

She had been vice-president of the British Society for Psychical Research for many years and had written extensively in the area, influencing, besides Koestler, Arnold Toynbee, the British historian, who included her careful essay on out-of-the-body experiences in his collection, *Man's Concern with Death*. But despite her absorption in the subject, she was suspicious of paranormal explanations for such curious phenomena. Like many other out-of-the-body researchers and subjects, she preferred to describe the phenomenon as an altered state of consciousness.

"I think the psychedelic drug experiences have been of enormous value to psychical research," she said, "because now a lot of people are able to envisage an altered state of consciousness, people who wouldn't have been able to thirty-six years ago when I joined the Society for Psychical Research."

As she spoke, she sat very still like a sibyl, and like a sibyl she spoke in riddles:

"I'm not sure that my 'white' me was necessarily within."

She meant that the out-of-the-body experience, although an altered state of consciousness, is not exclusively subjective—the paradox, also articulated by Palmer, which I kept running into during my investigation of the subject.

"A few years ago, there was a marvelous morning," she said. "I was down on an estuary in the south. My sister had a cottage right on the water. The sun was shining, the gulls were floating about, the water was sparkling, and so on. It was fabulously beautiful. Behind her cottage one walked up a tiny village street toward a twelfth-century church at the end, and there were flowers in the cottage gardens on each side. It really was an extraordinary morning. I remember I was stopped by a rose bush on the way up, and it was *so* fantastic that *that* got me out. Why the beauty got me out, I don't know. But I found myself—oh, dear, words!—caught up in what I can only describe as a larger consciousness, which held all the rest within. I found myself, so to speak, able to look down—you'll have to use the word *down*—as if from its point of view, and what I was looking down at was me. I was shocked. I don't know how long the experience lasted. I was so shaken by the intensity of it—I think the only word I can use is *awe* —that I thought I'd better creep up into the church where it would be silent and I could sit down and pull myself together.

"We don't have the words to describe what happens during an out-of-the-body experience, which is not quite the same thing as not having the concepts. Half the problem in trying to understand what is happening to us when we have these experiences is knowing what questions to ask. I'm not sure we ask the right questions."

Although Rosalind Heywood suggested that parapsychologists may have been asking the wrong questions, she didn't offer any specific proposals for what the "right questions" may be, questions which Dr. Harold Puthoff and Mr. Russell Targ, two lasar physicists at the Stanford Research Institute in Menlo Park, California, have been trying to determine. In 1972 and 1973 they ran a series of experiments with Ingo Swann, designed to test the range of his paranormal powers, which led them to wonder whether the "right questions" for psychical researchers to ask would focus, not on the paranormal experiences themselves, but on the nature of the reality in which the paranormal experiences existed.

In describing the results of their early work, which had concentrated on Swann's evident psychoenergetic gifts, one Stanford Research Institute news bulletin said:

> In the preliminary work, using a shielded magnetometer, Mr. Swann apparently demonstrated an ability to increase and decrease at will the magnetic field within a superconducting magnetic shield. The preliminary experiment made use of an existing facility, and SRI expressed confidence that Mr. Swann had no prior knowledge of either the apparatus or the intended experiment. "The experimental results have now been carefully scrutinized and are unlike any data previously produced with this apparatus," says SRI.
>
> In further preliminary work, Mr. Swann also demonstrated other apparent abilities, such as perceiving the location of and identification of objects hidden in containers.

On May 18, 1974, Russell Targ appeared at an American Society for Psychical Research Symposium, held at the Barbizon-Plaza Hotel in New York City. While describing SRI's out-of-the-body research (with Swann and others), he talked without expression, his left arm rigid at his side, his left hand flipping up and down like a dying fish on the end of a spear.

He explained that he called the phenomenon of describing a physical scene at a distance *"remote viewing, a non-evaluative term,"* because he did not like the phrase *out-of-the-body experience* and because he thought the label *astral projection*—even stripped of its Theosophical mythology—"has no semantic meaning at all."

In describing his findings he said, "One of the things we learned at first seemed paradoxical: the more difficult the task, the more likely we are to get success."

So rather than having a subject extend his awareness into another room or another building, Targ and his associates, following an experiment Ingo Swann designed, selected targets anywhere on earth and asked the subjects to describe the chosen place.

One of the more spectacular demonstrations occurred when Targ got a pair of geographical coordinates from the geographical division of the Stanford Research Institute and, without knowing himself where the spot was, asked Swann to describe what was there. Although fully conscious, puffing a cigar and drinking a cup of coffee, Swann reported the sensations associated with his out-of-the-body experience and described an island, drew a picture of it—indicating particular landmarks—and mentioned that the few people who lived on the island spoke French. The target was Kerguelen, a small island of about 1,300 square miles in the Indian Ocean, where the French had set up a meteorological station.

But I was disquieted by some aspects of the experiment. It seemed as bizarre to think that someone using "remote viewing" could locate a target by its geographical coordinates as it was to think that someone in his body, unaided, could locate a target by its geographical coordinates—although perhaps one of the powers of a "remote viewer" is a built-in sextant. Also, I was disturbed by the fact that Swann had suggested the experiment, a serious flaw in procedure which SRI had earlier recognized as such, stating in the above-quoted news release on the preliminary studies that SRI had "confidence that Mr. Swann had no prior knowledge of . . . the intended experiment." Targ offered no explanation of why, in these later experiments, he had allowed such a slip beyond saying that he had wanted a test which Swann would feel comfortable performing, a reasonable but hardly rigorous attitude. Swann's freedom to design the experiment left an opening for the kind of trickery that would not be impossible for someone with a photographic memory and a Hammond *Atlas*—an admittedly improbable theory. However, my tendency is to choose the least improbable of two astounding possibilities.

Still, Swann did sketch some details of the island, and memorizing aerial photographs of the entire planet would tax even the most clever memorist. The experiments were also tried successfully with other subjects —one of whom, a man called Price, was an ex-policeman from Burbank, California, who claimed to have used his psychic abilities to catch crooks. Even if Swann had been an extraordinary memorist, it is unlikely that the others possessed this remarkable power. So, tentatively, one could trust the experiments to be an authentic gauge of paranormal functions.

I also was bothered by Targ's suggested term, *remote viewing*, which muddied the semantic pool more than it clarified, by implying that the out-of-the-body function was only a kind of paranormal vision, which is not necessarily true. Or, if true of Swann, it may indicate that he was receiving distant information through a kind of clairvoyance, rather than showing that out-of-the-body perception such as that experienced by Blue Harary is limited to paranormal vision. Certainly, as Karlis Osis indicated, there is an important visual component to any out-of-the-body experience. But many out-of-the-body adepts, like Blue, have also reported out-of-the-body smelling, tasting, touching, and hearing. If Osis had concentrated on the visual aspect of the experience, it was to focus his experiments, not to exclude the other occasionally reported out-of-the-body senses. It is also possible that the out-of-the-body function operates as a kind of synesthesia, and the adept unconsciously isolates the particular sense most useful to describe the experience in terms of his in-body concepts of the world. Or the out-of-the-body function may be an entirely sense-less operation. Or it may involve senses of which we have no conception.

However it works, from the data gathered by SRI it appears that out-of-the-body functioning does not presuppose the loss of in-body control. Swann smoked cigars and sipped coffee while he was "remote viewing." This ability to perform normally in-body at the same time the subject is also having an out-of-the-body experience is a sign that, if the out-of-the-body experience is real, it is likely that consciousness extends but does not sever itself from the flesh.

Summing up his view of SRI's out-of-the-body studies, Targ said, "Both distance and time seem immaterial in this work. Consequently, in order to find an explanation we'll have to restructure our model of the space-time we live in."

If our model of space-time is inadequate to explain out-of-the-body experiences, any science rooted in that model may also be inadequate to study the phenomenon; and any effort to develop new conceptions of reality which would explain out-of-the-body experiences may necessitate new methods of scientific inquiry. Charles Tart, an associate professor of psychology at the University of California at Davis, feels that this is the essential problem facing all researchers—including those studying the out-of-the-body phenomenon—who are investigating non-ordinary states of consciousness.

CHAPTER 13

Toward A New Science

LIKE ROSALIND HEYWOOD, Puthoff, and Targ, Charles Tart sees psychical research, not as an esoteric backwater concerned with questions more appropriate to theology, but as a field capable of revolutionizing our view of the universe. He was interested in parapsychology before he was interested in psychology, and after receiving his B.A. in electrical engineering from the Massachusetts Institute of Technology in Cambridge, he decided to study psychology to acquire the necessary tools needed to do serious psychical research. In 1963 he got his Ph.D. in psychology from the University of North Carolina at Chapel Hill. After having completed post-doctoral research at Stanford University in California, he returned East to become an instructor in psychiatry at the University of Virginia School of Medicine in Charlottesville.

In 1965 he conducted some experiments with a woman who claimed to have experienced out-of-the-body sensations ever since she was a child. For four non-consecutive nights, her brain waves, eye movements, blood pressure, and skin resistance were monitored while she attempted to separate her consciousness from her body and, in her out-of-the-body state, move into another room and perceive a randomly chosen five-digit number which had been placed on a shelf that was about seven feet from the floor.

During the second experiment, Tart's subject woke at about 3:15 in the morning and told Tart to write down "3:13 A.M." After the experiment was over, she explained that she felt her consciousness had left her body and had moved into a position above the bed where she could see the clock. In the fourth experiment she woke at 6:04 A.M. and correctly identified the random five-digit number: 25232. Both of these incidents indicate that somehow Tart's subject appeared to be receiving information in a non-ordinary way at the same time that she had the sensations of being out of her body. However, because Tart could not absolutely rule out the possibility that she may have, consciously or unconsciously, picked up clues to the information she offered through her normal senses, he did not claim that these episodes provided conclusive proof for paranormal functioning.

Nevertheless, he did feel that the sessions had been valuable in studying the nature of out-of-the-body states. In "A Psychophysiological Study of Out-of-the-Body Experiences in a Selected Subject," published in the January, 1968, issue of *The Journal of the American Society for Psychical Research,* Tart reported that "it seems as if her out-of-the-body experiences occurred in conjunction with a non-dreaming, non-awake brain-wave stage characterized by predominant slowed alpha activity from her brain and no activation of the autonomic nervous system."

Later in the same year that Tart carried out this study, he ran a series of out-of-the-body experiments on a local businessman. The subject, whom Tart called Mr. X. in his report (published in the December, 1967, issue of *The International Journal of Parapsychology*), claimed to have had out-of-the-body experiences for many years; and Tart, using the same experiment he had designed for his first study, tested Mr. X.'s abilities.

Mr. X., wired to record his psychophysiological changes, was separated from the assisting technician and the electronic equipment by a glass window. During each test he would lie on a cot and try to extend his consciousness to a shelf which had been fixed above eye-level to a wall in the technician's monitor room and on which had been placed a random five-digit number that neither the technician nor the subject had seen. All the sessions were carried out at the University of Virginia hospital. Eight of them were conducted in the evening from nine o'clock to about midnight, and the ninth was an all-night study of sleep patterns.

Mr. X. failed to generate the sensation of leaving his body until the eighth session. After an hour of shifting around on the cot, distracted by the pain of the electrode clipped to his ear, he sat up and smoked a cigarette. When he lay down again, he tried with partial success to numb his earlobe. Then he concentrated on relaxing his body, one part at a time—toes, feet, calves, thighs. . . .

He felt the flush which he associated with the out-of-the-body experience, and he tried rolling out of his body, unsure—since the sensations of moving in the body and out of the body were so similar—if he was freeing himself from his flesh or dumping his physical self onto the floor. But he didn't crash from the cot; he was out-of-the-body.

He moved through a darkness into a lighted room where two men and a woman were seated on a couch. He couldn't hear them, and he wasn't able to attract their attention, so he opened his physical eyes and (back in his body) swallowed, closed his eyes, and floated out-of-the-body again, feeling himself spill from the cot, sink through the EEG wires, and bounce lightly on the floor.

He glided under the cot, his fingertips brushing the floor to keep his orientation, like a scuba-diver paddling along just above the sandy bottom of a cove. Poking into the technician's room, he glanced around without being able to find her; so he sailed out into the next room where the technician was standing with her husband. His ear started throbbing, and he swallowed to wet his throat with saliva. He sat up inside his physical body and called for the technician, who admitted, when he asked her, that she had left her post in the monitor room and had been in the next room talking to her husband.

In his report on the experiment, Tart said that Mr. X.'s EEGs were often remarkable, unlike common sleeping or waking patterns. His alpha rhythm frequency varied an unnaturally great degree from 8 to 13 cycles per second; and his

> sleep spindles ranged in frequency from 14 to 17 cps, 30 to 100 microvolts; almost every other subject I have seen in the laboratory has shown sleep spindles that were at 14 cps, and 14 cps only. Frequently, the theta waves in

his sleep patterns showed bursts of three to eight theta waves which had amplitudes of 150 to 200 microvolts; I have never seen theta activity in other subjects exceed about 50 microvolts.

Finally, although Mr. X. frequently fell asleep, I found no instances of clearly developed delta waves in any of his EEG patterns, whereas one generally sees delta waves within half an hour of falling asleep in all subjects. . . .

The question of whether Mr. X.'s OOBEs are "just" dreams cannot be answered definitely at present. I would tentatively hypothesize, however, that at least some of his OOBEs (such as the two in the laboratory) may be a *mixture* of dreaming and "something else." . . .

"We ought to drop the word *reality* and talk about *consensus reality*," Tart said, using a term similar to one Blue favored when I spoke with him. "We do shape each other's belief systems into mutually agreed upon illusions, and we act on those bases. One of the powers of science lies in its emphasis on open communication of data and consensual validation."

Consensual validation helps us to see through illusion —or at least to get enough agreement on the illusion for it to become a functional reality. One of the problems psychics and parapsychologists have always run into is that it is very difficult to get a fix on the unfamiliar realities they explore. Ingo Swann's visit to the constellation Sagittarius is a very private reality; it is hard under controlled laboratory conditions to validate it.

Although it might be predictable that most scientists cannot accept Swann's vision, the fact that out-of-the-body adepts also cannot accept each other's descriptions of the spaces they enter weakens their case. Swann's out-of-the-body world does not sound like

Blue's; Blue's does not sound like Rosalind Heywood's. These new worlds may be used emotionally and psychologically for the same purposes, but they do not at first glance appear to be the same place.

Tart suggested two explanations for this discrepancy. First, there may be only one out-of-the-body space, and the different reports could be the results of idiosyncratic interpretations.

"If I'm religious," said Tart, "and I see two people embracing on the street, I might see an obvious manifestation of brotherly love. If I'm not religious, I might figure those two people are horny."

Second, there may be many out-of-the-body spaces, and one's value system influences which of those spaces one enters when separated from the body.

"If you're religious in your body," said Tart, "you're more likely to walk into a church than if you're not. Where you go in the out-of-the-body state may be partly determined by chance and partly determined by where you want to go."

In either case the problem in trying to map the out-of-the-body universe remains. In "States of Consciousness and State-Specific Sciences," a paper Tart published in the June 16, 1972, issue of *Science,* the prestigious journal of the American Association for the Advancement of Science, he advocated that the tools of science, specifically consensual validation, could be applied to the study of altered states of consciousness— which he understood to include out-of-the-body experiences. He wrote:

> I now propose the creation of various state-specific sciences. If such sciences could be created, we would have a group of highly skilled, dedicated, and trained

practitioners able to achieve certain SoC's [states of consciousness], and able to agree with one another that they have attained a common state.

The trained observers would enter non-ordinary realities, look around, and report back what they found. If the observers had agreed upon a value system and a language ahead of time, any disagreement in their accounts of what they encountered would more likely be an indication that they had gone to different places, rather than that they had started out from different places. Any agreement in their accounts might be an indication that they had gone to the same place and that the place they went to had some kind of consistency.

Swann claimed he entered a psychic space where he perceived the constellation Sagittarius from a point of view outside of an earth-bound reference. If another observer went to that same space and saw Sagittarius in the same way it would suggest that their trips, psychic or literal, may have been authentic. SRI's experiment with a number of subjects guessing geographical coordinates was a version of this kind of test, and the indication that Price was able to duplicate some part of Swann's apparent success suggests that this attempt at achieving consensual validation may be fruitful. As soon as experimenters begin getting consensual validation, the argument is created that these experiences are not merely fantasies. Being and time may be more complex than Western man has traditionally assumed.

"I think our culture had a naive faith for the last several hundred years that there was some sort of rationality that transcended everything else," Tart said. "We thought we would get to that rationality, and all the spiritual stuff was just gross superstition. Well, it's not. The spiritual represents psychological and parapsychological realities that aren't going to go away. And they're not antagonistic to rationalism; they're just antagonistic to a narrow rationalism that thinks its arbitrary logic is the only way of seeing things.

"Rationality is only a tool, and you've got to be careful what you do with the tool. Abraham Maslow put it very beautifully once. He said, 'If the only tool you have is a hammer, you tend to treat everything as if it were a nail. That's great when you're working with nails. It's pretty bad when you've got to saw a piece of wood in half.'"

If the out-of-the-body experience is real, Tart's state-specific sciences would provide an opportunity to investigate *how* it is real, using a discipline which is a cross between science and a religion as fundamental as sympathetic magic. In sympathetic magic similar objects have power over each other. Like affects like. To kill a buffalo, you first shot an arrow into a picture of a buffalo. To escape from the cage of a narrow scientific rationalism, you use the tools of scientific rationalism. Like inoculating yourself against a disease with small amounts of the disease, we can best break down the assumptions of our often dysfunctioning consensus reality by using those assumptions against themselves. Using the accepted method of consensual validation, Tart's new state-specific scientists could travel to various other spaces and begin mapping those regions which, like the unexplored areas on medieval maps, are now filled with imaginary creatures and impossible places.

Tart's new science is, however, still an unrealized discipline. It's like a planned superhighway exit that has been marked, but not built. Until the time when his state-specific scientists can be trained and launched out of their bodies into the various unknown spaces that await them, we can only approach an explanation for the out-of-the-body phenomenon and the curious space-time it exists within through informed speculation, turning to theories which are rooted in both familiar and exotic realities.

PART 3

THEORISTS AND THEORIES

Unfortunately, the mythic side of man is given short shrift these days. He can no longer create fables. As a result, a great deal escapes him; for it is important and salutary to speak also of incomprehensible things. Such talk is like the telling of a good ghost story, as we sit before the fireside and smoke a pipe.

C. G. JUNG, *Memories, Dreams, Reflections*

CHAPTER 14

Psychoanalytic and Psychophysiological Theories

THE FIRST SIGNIFICANT psychoanalytic study of the experience of encountering the self was written by Otto Rank, an Austrian psychologist who studied with Freud and who, for a short time, was considered heir to Freud's kingdom of mind, until he broke with Freud in the early 1920s. Rank focused on the individual and creative aspects of personality, preferring to emphasize the differences rather than the similarities among people, and developing what came to be considered a functional, as opposed to a diagnostic, approach to therapy.

In 1914 Rank published the first version of his study of the phenomenon, *"Der Doppelgänger,"* an essay that he expanded into a book-length investigation and republished in 1925 as *Der Doppelgänger: Eine Psychoanalytische Studie.*

Rank regarded all forms of the double as related, and

he included in his examination such diverse phenomena as the sensation of seeing the physical self from a point of view outside the body, *doppelgängers*, symbolic representations of the self, split personalities, and mythic twins—all of which he described as aspects of the same complex psychic dodge. Nevertheless, his general theory can be tentatively applied to the specific event defined as an out-of-the-body experience.

In his book, he explained: "The most prominent symptom of the forms which the double takes is a powerful consciousness of guilt which forces the hero no longer to accept the responsibility for certain actions of his ego, but to place it upon another ego, a double. . . ."

This self-created double, which has become responsible "for certain actions of the ego," is an ambivalent creature, a target for either narcissistic longings or self-hatred, depending upon the circumstances under which it is encountered. As examples of both the benign and malevolent forms this double can take, Rank quoted two accounts of a self's interaction with its mirrored image. The first was taken from a newspaper item describing a contemporary trial:

> A young lord had locked up his beautiful, unfaithful sweetheart for eight days' punishment in a room whose walls consisted of panes of plate glass. . . . In the course of the days and nights which the young girl spent partly awake, she felt such a horror of the ever-recurrent image of her own face that her reason began to be confused. She continually attempted to avoid the reflection; yet from all sides her own image grinned and smiled at her. One morning, the old serving-woman was called in by a terrible rumpus: Miss R. was striking the reflecting walls with both fists; fragments were flying around and into

her face. . . . She kept on smashing, with only the purpose of no longer seeing the image of which she had conceived such a horror. . . ."

The second account, quoted from a historian named Edward Fuchs, describes how mirrors in "places of amorous activity" have been used to heighten eroticism:

> She was surprised by the marvel of seeing, without moving, her charming person in a thousand different ways. Her likeness was multiplied by the mirrors—thanks to an ingenious arrangement of the candles—and offered her a new spectacle, from which she was unable to avert her gaze.

These same reactions to the self's mirrored double are occasionally reported in accounts of out-of-the-body experiences, although self-love is more often described than self-loathing. In Yram's occult classic, *Practical Astral Projection*, a do-it-yourself handbook in which out-of-the-body experiences are interpreted as flights of an "astral" self from the flesh, the author struck a balance between the autoerotic and the autophobic:

> During another exercise . . . I became aware of myself by a definite slowing down of the breath, followed by the sensation of trying to squeeze through a narrow space. Then I felt more free and was no longer cramped. This time the room seemed rather dark. I contemplated without enthusiasm my physical body, whose shape showed through the bedcovers. I touched it; it seemed soft. I kissed myself and came away with the feeling of having kissed someone who had been dead only a short time.

Yram's reaction to himself, a flirtation that trembled on the edge of an autoerotic necrophilia, betrayed a fascination with the self and with death which is not uncommon to those who meet themselves or their doubles. Referring to Oscar Wilde's novel, *The Picture of Dorian Gray*, Rank linked these two fascinations: "One motif which reveals a certain connection between the fear of death and the narcissistic attitude is the wish to remain forever young."

And the wish to remain forever young generates an idealized image of the self, a soul which in most cultures is conceived of as being eternally youthful, uncorrupted by time. "The thought of death is rendered supportable by assuring oneself of a second life, after this one, as a double."

According to Rank, then, the out-of-the-body self, like a personalized secular Christ, is both a scapegoat, created to take responsibility for actions which the individual can no longer accept, and a soul-double, which assures the individual of a continuation of being after death. When the two theories are fused, Rank's argument forms a benign circle: the "powerful consciousness of guilt which forces the hero no longer to accept the responsibility for certain actions of the ego" becomes a universal guilt born of the realization that the self will someday die; and the specific action of the ego, which the self attempts to avoid responsibility for, is the ultimate action, the collaboration of each of us in our own inevitable death.

Half a decade after Rank published the first version of *"Der Doppelgänger,"* Sigmund Freud touched on the experience of seeing the self in his essay "The 'Uncanny.'"

He began his essay by describing an experience he had while traveling in a sleeping car on a train. The train jolted, and Freud mistook his own reflection in the mirror on the swinging door to the small washroom for a stranger gliding into his own compartment, a stranger whose looks he did not like at all.

Like Rank, Freud classified all the different experiences of encountering the self together, assuming that the experiences (all subjective) had a common root. And he presented the phenomena as examples of the uncanny, which occurs "either when repressed infantile complexes have been revived by some impression, or when the primitive beliefs we have surmounted seem once more to be confirmed."

When coincidence appears meaningful, for instance, it seems uncanny because it hints at the efficacy of sympathetic magic:

> As soon as something actually happens in our lives which seems to support the old, discarded beliefs, we get a feeling of the uncanny; it is as though we were making a judgment something like this: "So, after all, it is true that one can kill a person by merely desiring his death!" or, "Then the dead do continue to live and appear before our eyes on the scene of their former activities!" and so on.

If an out-of-the-body experience seems uncanny, it is because the conviction that one can separate his consciousness from his body may be a "primitive belief"— either true or false—which "we have surmounted" and which seems "once more to be confirmed."

The uncanny, however, is only the feeling—both familiar and unfamiliar at the same time—which surrounds an experience, not the experience itself. When analyzing the sensation of meeting the self, stripped of its uncanny aura, Freud first tipped his hat to Rank,

describing the creation of the double as a ploy to frus-
trate the annihilation of the ego that comes with death,
an act prompted by "primary narcissism."

But Freud followed this thought further, witnessing
the transformation the double undergoes in the developing personality:

> The idea of the "double" does not necessarily disap-
> pear with the passing of the primary narcissism, for it
> can receive fresh meaning from the later stages of devel-
> opment of the ego. A special faculty is slowly formed
> there, able to oppose the rest of the ego, with the func-
> tion of observing and criticizing the self and exercising
> a censorship within the mind, and this we become aware
> of as our "conscience" . . .
>
> The fact that a faculty of this kind exists, which is able
> to treat the rest of the ego like an object . . . renders it
> possible to invest the old idea of a "double" with a new
> meaning and to ascribe many things to it . . . all those
> unfulfilled but possible futures to which we still like to
> cling in phantasy, all those strivings of the ego which
> adverse external circumstances have crushed. . . .

The out-of-the-body self, then, under Freudian analysis, becomes a sensible projection of the conscience,
which is both a self-censor who demands autonomy in
order to accomplish its work and a focus for "all those
unfulfilled but possible futures to which we still like to
cling in phantasy. . . ." The out-of-the-body adept is only
someone who is compensating for the unfulfilled aspects of his life in reality by creating a second life in a
fantasy which he can control: Blue Harary, a withdrawn
friendless child, inhabits an out-of-the-body universe
that he shares with phantom friends; Tart's Mr. X., a
worldly businessman, takes refuge in an out-of-the-
body universe in which he engages in extravagantly
spiritual exercises.

If evidence of paranormal abilities were ignored, Freud's theory could rationalize some out-of-the-body episodes. Even if that evidence were not ignored, the theory could form a basis for understanding the type of narcissistic or frustrated personality most open to this particular kind of psychic phenomenon.

Unlike Rank and Freud, C. G. Jung dealt with the out-of-the-body experience directly, accepting it as a unique phenomenon in which consciousness appears to separate from the physical body. His responsiveness to the concept was partly a result of a personal episode.

In his autobiography, *Memories, Dreams, Reflections,* Jung described an experience he had early in 1944. After a heart attack, he had "a dream or an ecstasy" in which he felt as though his consciousness had extended itself outside of his body into space, where he looked down at the blue earth. As he turned his attention away from the planet, he perceived in space "a short distance away . . . a tremendous dark block of stone, like a meteorite," which had an entrance that led into its hollow interior.

> To the right of the entrance, a black Hindu sat silently in lotus posture upon a stone bench . . . Innumerable tiny niches, each with a saucer-shaped concavity filled with coconut oil and small burning wicks, surrounded the door. . . .
>
> As I approached the steps leading up to the entrance . . . I had the feeling that everything was being sloughed away . . . the whole phantasmagoria of earthly existence . . . fell away or was stripped from me. . . . I had the certainty that I was about to meet the people who knew the answer . . . about what had been before and what would come after . . .

But, like a scene in a serialized adventure movie, the episode ended with a cliff-hanger. Jung's doctor called him back to earth, and Jung "profoundly disappointed . . . thought, 'Now, I must return to the "box system" again.' "

While Jung was unconscious, or in an altered state of consciousness, his nurse noticed that he was " 'surrounded by a bright glow' . . . which was a phenomenon she had sometimes observed in the dying."

His near-death experience was similar to both the deathbed visions that Karlis Osis had studied and to the out-of-the-body states reported by Blue Harary and Ingo Swann: he perceived as though his out-of-the-body consciousness were a disembodied ego; he encountered intelligent presences in his out-of-the-body world; and he floated, if not to the constellation Sagittarius, at least into earth orbit.

Although the event was fantastic, Jung was convinced it was not a fantasy. In talking about both his out-of-the-body experience and certain subsequent visions, he categorized them as being "utterly real" and explained them as moments when the self is fulfilled, when a person completes a process of psychic growth, when one accidentally stumbles into the eternal.

"The objectivity which I experienced . . . in the visions is part of a completed individuation," Jung said. "It signifies detachment from valuations and from what we call emotional ties."

Everything which ties a person to an earth-bound ego, especially affects, are in part products of our projections, and "it is essential to withdraw these projections in order to attain to oneself and to objectivity." The process of becoming more and more oneself is, Jung suggests, in some way equal to the process of per-

ceiving the world with complete objectivity, unham-
pered by emotional ties. "Objective cognition lies hidden behind the attraction of the emotional relationship;
it seems to be the central secret."

Since the world is colored by the way we feel about
it, to experience "objective cognition" would be
equivalent to seeing reality without any illusions, from
the point of view of a disinterested god. To achieve
such a passionless perspective, one must continually
"withdraw projections." But as old illusions and misconceptions about the world are destroyed, new illusions
and misconceptions may take their place. The meteorite temple, the Hindu, the eternal company which Jung
expected to meet in the belly of the huge dark block
may have been a new phantasmagoria, created from
Jung's imagination to replace the old "phantasmagoria
of earthly existence"—an illusory reality as much a
product of projections as the world Jung left on earth.

Jung's out-of-the-body experience could have been
real, but all the stage sets, all the props that furnished
the experience could have been illusions. Had Jung
pushed further and further toward "the central secret,"
destroying one set of illusions after another, he may
have found that, to some extent, all reality is a product
of our projections, and objective cognition, if it were
possible to attain, would be an awful void, an absence,
a world without form.

Jung described this state outside space and time as
"trans-psychic reality," and he identified it as the condition in which paranormal events occurred. In a letter
written in May of 1960, which Aniela Jaffé quoted in her
book, *From the Life and Work of C. G. Jung,* Jung
explained:

The comparative rarity of such phenomena suggests at all events that the forms of existence inside and outside time are so sharply divided that crossing this boundary presents the greatest difficulties. But this does not exclude the possibility that there is an existence outside time which runs parallel with existence inside time. Yes, we ourselves may simultaneously exist in both worlds, and occasionally we do have intimations of a twofold existence. But what is outside time is, according to our understanding, outside change. It possesses relative eternity.

Jung's model leads to a theory that during an out-of-the-body experience one perceives both this reality and "trans-psychic reality" from the viewpoint of the second component of our "twofold existence." But the "relatively" eternal is outside the scope of scientific analysis. Any investigation of the paranormal must limit itself to observations from this side of the boundary separating "existence inside and outside time." In his essay "Synchronicity: An Acausal Connecting Principle," which was published in 1952 and revised and translated into English in 1955, Jung attempted to explain the out-of-the-body phenomenon from the standpoint of an observer inside time, using a theory that would not violate any of the laws of a time-bound universe.

He described a near-death experience in which a woman, unconscious and bleeding extensively as a result of a difficult birth, accurately perceived herself, the hospital room she was in, the doctor, the nurse, and her relatives, as though her consciousness had fixed itself at a point in the ceiling and was looking down at the activity around her bed.

Jung dismissed the idea that she was actually semiconscious and hysterically fantasizing a dissociated awareness. Accepting the phenomenon as a real event, Jung suggested that "during a coma the sympathetic [nervous] system is not paralyzed and could therefore be considered as a possible carrier of psychic functions."

This theory, while attractively rationalistic, fails to explain why the sympathetic nervous system would seem to organize sensory information from a point outside the body as though the "eyes were in the ceiling."

A year after Jung first published his essay on synchronicity, Caro W. Lippman published "Hallucinations of Physical Duality in Migraine" in the *Journal of Nervous and Mental Diseases* (Volume 117). In this article, Lippman indicated that the "sensation of physical duality, during which such mental qualities as observation, judgment, perception, etc., are transferred to 'the other,' or 'second body' . . . usually lasts for a few seconds, coming and going before, during, or after" the migraine. Sometimes, he said, it can occur days before the attack; other times the hallucination can appear among those he called *migrainoids*, "the sons and daughters of parents who suffer from classic migraine headaches."

Although Lippman drew no conclusions, by merely offering evidence of a relationship between migraines and out-of-the-body sensations, he hinted that both phenomena had related organic causes.

In "The Double: Its Psychopathology and Physiology," an article written by John Todd and Kenneth Dewhurst and published in the *Journal of Nervous and Mental Diseases* (1955, Volume 122), the authors offered a stew of theories, drawn from Rank, Freud, Jung, and neurology. They suggested that autoscopy could be a result of narcissism; extraordinary powers of visualization; archetypal thinking (conceptualizing in symbols drawn not from the personal, but from the collective unconscious); and "irritative lesions in the somatognostic areas of the brain," those sections of the brain which govern everything from the primary sensations like pain, heat, and pressure to self-image, general bodysense, and specific awareness of the body in relationship to the rest of the world—an assumption that would not necessarily contradict Lippman's conception of the connection between autoscopy and migraine.

N. Lukianowicz (in "Autoscopic Phenomena," an article published in the August, 1958, issue of the *A.M.A. Archives of Neurology and Psychiatry*, Volume 80, Number 2) noted that autoscopy appeared related not only to migraines but also to epilepsy. He made a distinction between symptomatic (organically caused) and idiopathic (psychogenically caused) autoscopy, interpreting the first type as the result of "a known organic causation," possibly "some irritating process in the temporoparietal lobes," and the second type as the result of "a compensatory or a wish-fulfilling mechanism." He also related autoscopy to

> such parahallucinatory phenomena as imaginary companions, eidetic [vivid and unreal] images, self-appearances, clairvoyance, hypnagogic imagery, and some "anatomically incomplete" body image disturbances, such as phantom limb and the group of delusional reduplication of parts of the body.

In his article on autoscopy in *Tōhoku Psychologica Folia* (1960), Serio Kitamura judged the phenomenon to be a hallucination during which the body is usually imagined as shorter than it really is if the subject has his eyes open and as larger than it really is if the subject is blind.

Although the connection between autoscopy and migraine was supported by my research—many of the people I talked with who experienced out-of-the-body sensations also suffered from migraine—neither that observation nor any of the other psychophysiological observations or theories explained away the evidence of paranormal powers which are often manifest in out-of-the-body episodes; and since in each of these discussions the phenomenon was assumed to be something other than what it was experienced to be, these traditional interpretations are best accepted as metaphors, useful fictions. They can help us understand the psychophysiological conditions which are likely to produce out-of-the-body experiences, just as the theories of Rank, Freud, and Jung can help us understand the psychological conditions under which the phenomenon can occur.

One of the more common psychological and psychophysiological conditions which can trigger the out-of-the-body experience is the near-death state, brought on either by an accident, as in the case of Bob Hall or Jung, or in the normal course of a fatal illness. In 1970 Dr. Russell Noyes, Jr., a University of Iowa psychiatrist, started collecting descriptions of near-death episodes with the intention of putting together a map of the moment of dying. While gathering material, he kept coming across accounts in which people reported the feeling that their consciousness had left their physical body, descriptions that greatly interested him.

"I'm a pretty straight sort of fellow as you can see,"

Noyes said. "I'd never really ventured off into the parapsychological, and this particular thing with the mystical dying experience is a kind of far-out thing for me."

Dwelling on death can have the same effect on a nervous system as learning not to blink while sticking a contact lens into an eye, and Noyes displayed that fixed openness which invited trust and discouraged familiarity. He spoke hesitantly about his work, aware that he had intruded on a field in which it is impossible to gather altogether trustworthy data because it is hard for people to discuss near-death experiences without skidding into speculation on death. Death can only be perceived by its reflection in life, as though it were a curled hair which, floating invisibly on the brightly lit surface of tub water, casts a shadow on the enameled tub bottom.

Ever since he was a boy in Bloomington, Indiana, Noyes had been curious about death from a non-mystical point of view. He cultivated this detached passion at DePauw University, at Indiana University Medical School, and at Philadelphia General Hospital, where he interned.

"There was a young man who had a small tumor in his chest," Noyes said. "We did surgery and found that it was inoperable cancer. I felt that when he awoke I should inform him of what we had found, but I discovered myself feeling quite fearful in confronting him. In fact, I told him nothing. Surprisingly enough, he asked me nothing. We never spoke about what was the most obvious thing."

That experience focused his interest in death and dying. He began digging into the literature on the subject and discovered that often dying was reported as a subjectively pleasant experience during which the conscious mind seemed dissociated from the failing body.

"I also began looking for cases among the people who came to me here at the University," said Noyes.

One twenty-five-year-old racing car driver who was involved in two potentially fatal accidents in the late spring and early summer of 1971, described for Noyes a collision on a racetrack in Knoxville, Iowa, which flipped his super-modified sprint car thirty feet in the air:

> Everything was in slow motion, and it seemed to me like I was a player on a stage. I could see myself tumbling over and over in the car. It was as though I sat in the stands and saw it all happen. . . . I saw flashes of colors. I distinctly remember blues, greens, and yellows. Everything was so strange. . . . I remember being upside down and looking backwards. And I saw the man who won the race pass under me. The guy looked up, and I remember that he had an amazed look on his face.

After reading of Noyes's work, a seventy-nine-year-old woman contacted him about a near-drowning experience she'd had when she was thirteen during a vacation at an artificial lake in Paris, Illinois. She wrote:

> The area skirting the shore was shallow, but dropped quickly into a deep channel. I didn't know how to swim. . . . Suddenly one of the group slipped into the channel. As I reached for her, I slipped into the channel myself. My head was under water. Feeling her long hair, I caught ahold of it and pulled. I knew the shallow water was only a step or two away, but I could not find it immediately. At that moment I felt no fear. I had no appreciation of the urgent crisis. It was all so instantaneous. I knew death was imminent. At that point a series of clear pictures appeared before me. I recognized them

as the complete replaying of the events in my life in proper sequence. They appeared in a flash. Each was framed and distinct.

In this account, as in many others which Noyes gathered, it is hard to separate the sensation of actually being outside the body and perceiving a life-review from the sensation of having the life-review flash through one's imagination. This discrepancy could be due to differing interpretations of a single experience: someone who is open to paranormal belief may feel he has actually left his body even if he hasn't; someone who is closed to paranormal belief may feel out-of-the-body sensations are merely subjective fantasies even if they aren't. Or there may be two distinct experiences: one normal and subjective, in which someone has the sensation of reliving past experiences; the other paranormal and objective, in which someone, ripped from his physical body and existing temporarily outside of our traditional concepts of time and space, actually perceives his past spread out for him as though "on a stage."

Noyes did not differentiate between the two interpretations. Any feeling of a consciousness dissociated from the physical body, according to him, was a result of an altered state of awareness, which could be triggered by drugs, sensory deprivation, or exhaustion as well as by near-death episodes.

"I think they're experiencing a different level of consciousness," Noyes said about people who report out-of-the-body sensations. "Now what interpretation to place on that is something I can't say. One day I went to see a patient. She had a serious physical illness. She was delirious. I asked her what date it was and where she was. She said, 'I'm half in heaven and half on earth.' There was a lustrous look in her eyes, and she had a rapturous smile. She looked far off as though she was having grand visions and was in ecstasy. I asked her what it was like up there, naturally. And I was disappointed. She said, 'There's a lot of people, and there's a lot of work to do.' I said I thought it sounded just like it was down here.

"I like to look at this kind of experience as regression. When a person regresses, there is a reversion to more childlike ways of behaving, and there's a conservation of energy involved. Anyone who gets sick regresses. His sphere of interest shrinks. He takes less responsibility for things about him. He depends more on others. He's less autonomous. His energy is conserved. Now, if this process were to move rapidly to some kind of completion, one might think that there would be some sort of discharge of energy. It seems to me that most of us have quite an involvement in our future, and if you deprive a person of that, there'd be really a tremendous redirection of that energy."

Noyes stopped short of explaining precisely how or why this redirection of energy would elicit the sensations of being outside the body, but he implied that it would be through perfectly normal means. One didn't have to abandon Western culture's generally accepted version of the world to account for it. Because Noyes avoided any consideration of evidence for paranormal phenomena associated with the dissociation of consciousness from the physical body, his theory—like other traditional psychoanalytic and psychophysiological speculation—was incomplete.

If the out-of-the-body phenomenon is real, and if it is a paranormal event, any analysis limited to this side of the boundary separating what Jung called "existence inside and outside time" can only be wanting. It may be impossible to formulate what Rosalind Heywood called "the right questions" within our familiar sciences. To track down the phenomenon it may be necessary to deal with the world outside time and to entertain, at least temporarily, more esoteric theories than those to be found in everyday reality.

CHAPTER 15

Esoteric Theories

ONE OF THE CLASSIC ESOTERIC THEORIES of the out-of-the-body experience can be found in the books of Robert Crookall, who has been publishing his thoughts on the subject since 1960. Crookall, a former paleobotanist with the British Geological Survey, was born in 1890 in Lancaster, England. Shortly before Hornell Hart died, he noted Crookall's work in a paper for the March, 1967 (Volume 9), issue of the *International Journal of Parapsychology* in which he said, "Dr. Robert Crookall's collections raised the study of out-of-body cases to a new level of comprehensiveness."

The books *are* comprehensive, listing hundreds of accounts; but although he is widely respected as a compiler, the value of his theories is questionable. His explanations were rooted in the same occult tradition that produced Fox, Yram, and Muldoon; he believed in the

stock of props which that tradition used to explain out-
of-the-body phenomena—multiple bodies, silver cords,
a universe layered like baklava with astral planes—although he quibbled about the specific nature of the
concepts.

Traditional Theosophy pulled seven bodies from the
self, like a child opening up an accordion-cut paper doll:
a physical body; an etheric double, which is also physical; an astral body; a mental body; a causal body, which
functions in the same plane as the mental body; a
spiritual body; and the buddhic.

Crookall recognized only four bodies: the physical
body; the vehicle of vitality, which has no awareness
and which is the *vardøger*, the *doppelgänger*, the *tàslach*, and the *tamhasg*; the soul body, which has a consciousness and which is responsible for incidents of
telepathy, precognition, clairvoyance; and the cosmic
body, which is eternal and which is united with the All.

Crookall agreed with Theosophy that each body fit
into a neat spiritual niche. But Theosophists identified
seven planes, one for each body, while Crookall argued
that there were only four. Both Theosophy and Crookall admitted that the categories were not fixed. In *The
Astral Body*, an occult work published in 1927, A. E.
Powell said: "The matter of each sub-plane interpenetrates that of the sub-plane below it: consequently, at
the surface of the earth, all seven sub-planes exist together in the same space. . . ."

As one rises from one plane to another, like a balloon-
ist casting off ballast, he shucks each of his denser bodies
until the last body (which, I suppose, would be the
balloon) is gone and all that is left is air.

Theosophists also insisted on the reality of the astral
cable, which is an umbilical cord connecting the physi-

cal body to the out-of-the-body self, a figment popular among most occultists and often borrowed from the Theosophists. Sylvan Muldoon described the cable as being like an elastic cord. In *The Projection of the Astral Body* (first published in 1929), Muldoon said:

> The less space that lies between the two bodies the greater is the thickness of the astral cable. . . . When slightly out of coincidence, the cord is the diameter of a silver dollar. . . . The diameter decreases in proportion to the increase of separation of the bodies, up to a given distance . . . its calibre then being that of an ordinary sewing thread. . . .

Some occultists see the physical body as the generator of a life force that energizes the out-of-the-body self, which roars off like an electric motorcycle, trailing a line-cord behind it. Others, like Muldoon and Crookall, see the physical body as being animated by a charge traveling through the astral cable, which is plugged into some ultimate source of power. But Muldoon said, "where it comes from, on the outgoing of the phantom, where it disappears, when the phantom coincides [with the physical body], are too deep mysteries for me to fathom."

Crookall, although as modest in his approach to the phenomenon as Muldoon, tried to delve deeper; and he untwined two cords from one.

"If a man is dying, you might see a cord attached to the navel," he said, as he sat in the small living room of his apartment in Bath, England. "If he is not, you might see a cord attached at the head. If there are two cords, that would suggest there are two bodies which can separate from the physical. The fourth body, the spiritual or cosmic body, has no form; it just is."

Crookall was logical, deducing facts about the out-of-the-body phenomenon from questionable premises which he accepted as true. At the center of his argument was the syllogism: If consciousness cannot exist without a body, and if people report the sensation of having a disembodied consciousness, then there must be a disembodied body which acts as a carrier for that disembodied consciousness.

Although Crookall's theory was esoteric, he was a rationalist, and the unreality of his argument was due in great part to applying a nineteenth-century materialist's logic to what may have been an inappropriate question. He collected his hundreds of cases with the same thoroughness he, as a paleobotanist, had gathered plant fossils, convinced that with enough intelligent study man could crack all the secrets of the universe, including those that dealt with death.

"People experience two deaths," he explained. "In the first death both out-of-the-body bodies are above the physical body, but the soul body is enshrouded by the vehicle of vitality. Then the vehicle of vitality drops away. When someone has an out-of-the-body experience, he might be in both or only in the soul body. That explains why sometimes a man will leave his body and can pass through a wall and another time he can't. It's all a lot of nonsense—until you see what the key is."

The key to Crookall's philosophy, of course, was a belief in a life after death. His out-of-the-body theory was essentially religious; and like most nineteenth- and twentieth-century occult visions of the world, it was a desperate attempt to develop a new rationale for failing Western religion. Because the main stream of Western thought has become, in its growing materialism, inhospitable to religion, those who try to save the

spiritual are forced outside the culture in their search
for a cure. But in trying to make their new-found alien
ideas acceptable to Western culture, they must interpret them in terms the culture can understand; and in
that process of translation they become trapped into
using the very tools that have destroyed what they're
trying to save. This tragic confusion that saps the energies of occultists is a reflection, in small, of Western
thought at the end of its tether, monomaniacally trying
to wed rationalism to the sacred, unable to accept the
results of three hundred years of its own logic.

According to many esoteric theories, including Crookall's, the aura is that substance which extends or separates from the body and which encases the perceiving
out-of-the-body intelligence. And like a procession of
comic book ghosts, all colored outlines around voided
centers, the various versions of the aura glide through
any discussion of the out-of-the-body experience: the
glow around the Hindu Devas, the halos surrounding
Christian saints, the radiance circling Jung when he lay
half-dead in his hospital bed, the astral body which,
according to Crookall, hangs like a mist about three-
quarters of an inch from the skin, the etheric body
which, according to spiritualist tradition, extends one-
quarter to one-half inch from the skin and weighs two-
and-one-half ounces.

In 1845 Baron Karl Ludwig von Reichenbach, one of
the first chemists to study the properties of solid par-
affin, published the results of his experiments with sen-
sitives who claimed to see vapors streaming from mag-
nets, reddish-yellow around the south pole, bluish-
green around the north pole. Von Reichenbach related
this "odic force" to the magnetic fluids which Mesmer-

ists described as passing between subject and hypnotist; and he explained that in humans the odic force blazed from the fingertips.

About half a century later, Nikola Tesla, the electrical engineer who made practical the use of alternating current, took photographs in the high-frequency energy-field generated by the Tesla coil (which he had invented) that showed rays flaring from the human body.

Around the same time Navratil, a Czech, Nipher, an American, Baraduc, a Frenchman, and Narkevich-Todko, a Russian, were also experimenting with what Navratil had called electrophotography. And in 1911 Dr. Walter J. Kilner, a doctor at St. Thomas' Hospital in London, England, published his book, *The Human Atmosphere,* which detailed his experiments using dicyanine-dyed screens and goggles to make visible the aura which he insisted surrounded the human body. Dicyanine was a dye used to sensitize photographic plates to red rays. The viewer would stare through the specially prepared glass first directly at a light, then at a naked subject who was positioned twelve inches in front of a black background.

Kilner reported three distinct auras: the inner envelope about one- to three-sixteenths of an inch wide and transparent; the middle envelope about two to four inches wide and granulated; and the outer envelope, a glowing egg, which had no distinct outline and which gradually dissolved into the surrounding space. Women and children under thirteen had finer auras than men, and the woman's aura was wider around the waist than the man's aura. Intelligent subjects had expanded auras around the head. Gray auras indicated dullness.

Kilner also identified three kinds of rays emanating from the body: patches of light within the aura; streams of brilliant color connecting different parts of the body; and flares that shot out at right angles to the body. The auras and the rays varied in width and color according to the psychological and physiological states of the subjects; and certain subjects learned how to control their auras and rays using their will, like Marvel Comics heroes zapping the villains with shafts of light which flash from their fingers.

In 1939 in the *Journal of the Biological Photographic Association* (Volume 7), two Czech scientists, Dr. Silvester Prat and Dr. Jan Schlemmer, outlined their investigations into electrophotography, which had produced pictures of leaves surrounded by auras. In the same year Wilhelm Reich, one of Freud's early associates, stated that he had discovered what he called "cosmic orgone energy," which existed universally, penetrated all matter, and manifested itself (among its other forms) as electricity, lightning, magnetism, gravity, and the aurora borealis.

Orgone energy could be seen both as a blue aura and as a free-floating blue glow; it was the life-force, which sought to know itself. In *Cosmic Superimposition*, first published in 1951, Reich said: "The quest for knowledge expresses desperate attempts, at times, on the part of the orgone energy within the living organism to comprehend itself, to become conscious of itself. . . ."

And Reich's description of this impulse toward self-revelation evoked the out-of-the-body phenomenon: "This burning urge to know can be felt like a stretching of our senses beyond the material framework of our body. . . ."

In the same year that Prat and Schlemmer made public their work and that Reich announced his discovery of orgone energy, a Russian electrician, Semyon D.

Kirlian, started taking pictures of objects placed directly on photographic paper within a high-frequency field. His results were extraordinary: surrounding a fingertip were flares and auras like those Kilner had seen through his treated goggles, and bubbles and droplets that looked like the "bions" which Reich had claimed were the basic units of all living matter. A leaf which had been cut still showed an aura outlining the space where the missing part would have been; in a withering leaf the aura and flares dimmed and vanished.

Kirlian summed up his research in "Photography by Means of High-Frequency Currents" (written with his wife, Valentina, and published in an English translation in *The Kirlian Aura,* an anthology of articles on Kirlian's work, edited by Stanley Krippner and Daniel Rubin, which appeared in 1974):

> Our work showed that in a high-frequency field, auto-electron and auto-ion emission is characteristic of all bodies of nature including living organisms. . . .
>
> The electrical structure of a living organism is not constant, because it depends on its condition at any given moment. All changes in the course of its life processes are accompanied by changes in its dielectric system. . . .
>
> By studying the geometric figures, their spectrum and dynamics of development, it will be possible to judge the biological state of an organism and its organs including disease and pathology.

Kirlian's aura, like Reich's orgone energy, seemed to radiate from all living things, and, like Kilner's triple-halos, varied according to the health of the life-form being photographed.

After visiting the Soviet Union to examine Kirlian techniques in use at Kirov State University of Kazakhstan in Alma-Alta, Dr. Thelma Moss, a professor at the Neuropsychiatric Institute of the University of California at Los Angeles, tested a similar process in America with Ken Johnson. They summarized their procedure in "Radiation Field Photography," published in the July, 1972, issue of *Psychic*. Instead of working with a Tesla coil, as had the Kirlians, they worked with an apparatus that "uses a far *lower* (and safer) frequency of 3000 hertz (cycles per second). And instead of two plates sandwiching the object, our apparatus has been simplified to operate with one plate and an insulated grounding wire." They also suggested that by employing these methods "the out-of-the-body experience could at last be studied by photographic means."

A coronal discharge created by an electrical current passing through an object is not necessarily evidence of an energy body; but an energy body is a serviceable construct, connecting many mysterious phenomena such as Kirlian's electrobioluminescence, astral bodies, halos, even acupuncture points (which seem to correspond to the spots on the body that, under Kirlian photography, show the brightest flares)—all can be wrapped in a neat package if one entertains the possibility of an energy body.

That attractive, although occult, assumption was made in 1968 by six reputable Russian scientists— V.M. Inyushin (whom Moss had talked with when she visited Russia), V.S. Grishchenko, N. Vorobev, N. Shouiski, N. Fedorova, and F. Gibadulin—after a series of experiments in which they used Kirlian's techniques to photograph a wide variety of objects. In "The Biological Essence of the Kirlian Effect" (a

paper published by the State University of Kazakhstan and quoted in Sheila Ostrander's and Lynn
Schroeder's *Psychic Discoveries Behind The Iron
Curtain*) the six Russians claimed that the aura visible under Kirlian photography was a unified organism with its own electromagnetic fields; they called
this organism the Biological Plasma Body.

Noting the Russians' research, Dr. William A. Tiller,
a professor of materials science at Stanford University
in California who visited Russia to explore Kirlian photography in 1971, sketched a working hypothesis to explain such odd phenomena in "Devices for Monitoring
Nonphysical Energies," a paper published in 1974 in
Edgar D. Mitchell's and John White's collection, *Psychic Exploration*. Tiller is a government consultant in
metallurgy, chemistry, and solid state physics who has
published more than one hundred scientific papers and
two books; he is no fringe occultist. Like a man entering
a dark, vaguely familiar room, he worked his way into
a theory which postulated that

> . . . the human body is constituted of seven different
> types of substances that obey seven unique sets of natu-
> ral laws and, based on the polarity principle, form atomic
> and other states of combinations at each level of sub-
> stance. From these different levels of substance, differ-
> ent types of radiations emanate.

Science, it seems, can slip into alignment with
Theosophy as easily as an etheric body slips into coincidence with the physical self.

Six years before Inyushin and his colleagues publi-
cized the Biological Plasma Body and nearly a decade
before Tiller went to Russia to study Kirlian's discover-

ies, an American neurologist, Dr. Andrija Puharich, working outside the field of electrophotography, introduced in his book *Beyond Telepathy* the concept of "psi-plasma," an envelope surrounding material bodies.

Puharich theorized that during states of adrenergia (excitement, shock, terror, anxiety) the human body exerts an increased gravitational attraction which causes the psi-plasma field to contract, and that during states of cholinergia (relaxation, pleasure, extreme calm) the human body exerts a decreased gravitational attraction which causes the psi-plasma field to expand. The increased gravitational attraction of someone in a state of adrenergia can draw a weakly held psi-plasma field from someone in a state of cholinergia, connecting the two bodies.

This, Puharich explained, is the basic principle behind all paranormal phenomena. Out-of-the-body experiences, telepathy, clairvoyance, psychokinesis, and precognition. All, inextricably united, are aspects of a single phenomenon, and it is not possible to understand one without examining the others. Although Puharich joins all paranormal phenomena, he still sees each odd power operating in a specific way. In an out-of-the-body experience, for example, it is the psi-plasma field which, expanded beyond the body, perceives, sometimes organizing its information as though the perception were visual in order to give it a form that would be easily interpreted. In telepathy and clairvoyance information is transmitted through the pseudopod that joins one psi-field to another. In psychokinesis the extended psi-plasma field is the agent of the interaction between the psychic and the object being influenced. And in precognition what seems to be knowledge of the future is an interchange, partly psychokinetic, between psi-plasma and matter-energy fields.

> . . . all material bodies have a psi-plasma field. . . . All psi-plasma fields are probably continually interacting and being influenced. Therefore the net effect of any psi-plasma field on a matter-energy field will be based on a probability. . . . Each individual has a small vote that can exert its small quantum of mental action on the over-all psi-plasma field.

An individual powerfully exerting telergic effects on his psi-plasma field could possibly tip the "vote" one way or another, influencing the future event, giving the impression that he knew ahead of time what that event would be.

Puharich's model, developed from observations about the neurology of various altered and paranormal states of consciousness, gives off its own aura of well-reasoned, simple authority. *Beyond Telepathy* is a serious attempt to put together a general theory of the paranormal, the result of more than a decade of searching through the unknown, which started when a friend idly mentioned telepathy to him in December, 1947.

"I was a typical know-it-all young scientist, finishing up my residency in neurophysiology at the Kaiser Permanente Hospital in Oakland, California," said Puharich. "I wanted some evidence that telepathy existed. So I decided to give myself a two-year sabbatical to find out if it did."

The two years lengthened to seven. Puharich studied ESP with Eileen Garrett, the most respected medium of the twentieth century, and with psychics Peter Hurkos and Harry Stone. In 1954 he became interested in the consciousness-altering properties of the mushroom *amanita muscaria,* and during research in the subject he began running across descriptions of the out-of-the-body experience.

"I didn't get too excited about it at first," said Puharich, "because it was an uncontrollable situation. And then I had my own out-of-the-body experience."

On the afternoon of December 13, 1954, Puharich lay down to take a nap. After falling immediately asleep, he realized he was floating on the ceiling and staring down at his body which was sprawled fully clothed on the bed. He thought that he should get to Mrs. Garrett, feeling that since she was a medium, she might be able to perceive his disembodied body and possibly offer some kind of proof that he was not dreaming. And as though the thought had recreated his world, he found himself in Mrs. Garrett's New York apartment. But like a child trying to attract the attention of a figure on a television screen, he was unable to communicate with her. After launching himself into another room and trying unsuccessfully to contact another friend, he gave up; and he slipped back into his body like smoke going down a chimney in a film run backwards.

"For the first time in my life I realized that there was a duality," Puharich said. "I was trained not to believe in a duality, there was something unaesthetic about it; but I realized that in the case of the human consciousness there is a part which is the real perceiver, the experiencer, the analyzer that exists independently of the body and says, 'Jesus, that was a nice pair of clothes I was wearing this trip, but the real me is here, the other thing has got no life in it.' "

During the late 1950s he continued to study the ability of hallucinogenics to boost psi-effects, and in 1960 he led a fourteen-man expedition into Oaxaca, Mexico, to root out whatever psychedelic truffles they could find. The project was sponsored by the United States Army Chemical Corps, the University of Washington, and the Aluminum Company of America, an alliance which is not as unlikely as it seems at first: the military-educational-industrial hydra nodding three of its heads in unison.

Throughout the next few years Puharich roamed the world. In Hawaii, where he unearthed *Paneolus Campanulatus,* the first hallucinogenic mushroom to be found there, he was initiated into the native Kahuna religion, one of whose rites involved going out-of-the-body to other parts of the Islands.

Like most people who have experienced the out-of-the-body state, Puharich had developed his own language to explain what he went through. He preferred to call that which separated from the physical body "a mobile center of consciousness"; the physical body was merely a convenient shell, a temporary stopping place for that mobile center of consciousness.

"The reality of myself is not my body," he said. "If I amputate my leg, it doesn't mean a goddamn thing. That's not me at all, that's not the real me. The mobile center of consciousness is the thing that survives, that goes on and on and will find another body, another existence—and so it goes through the evolutionary chain. I don't know where it started or where it's going, but I'm sure there are infinite different existences, different realities. And we have to master each of those realities before going on to the next.

"The physical body is just a piece of clothing that you have to take care of, 'cause if you don't the soul

won't have its proper playground to work out in.
When you're in an earth life, you may have to recy-
cle here a few times—reincarnation—before you go
on to the next state, whatever that may be. It may
be in an anti-matter world; it may be in a world
made up of sixty-two atoms. We on earth in this life
may be in the middle of that whole sequence, the
beginning, I don't know."

Puharich was one of the most difficult parapsychologists to judge. He was obviously clever. He possesses
fifty-six U.S. and international patents and has worked
as part of a New York University Medical Center team
to create—modest Frankenstein—an artificial heart.
But he also juggled psychics, flying saucers, outrageous
occult notions, Theosophical conceits, Zen beliefs, and
Western science like a circus clown tossing around Indian clubs while balancing on a high-wire. His en-
thusiasms were promiscuous. Accepting a mobile center of consciousness is one thing; believing, as he does,
in fifth-dimensional—or nth-dimensional—UFOs is another.

The problem could be that he had an inadequate
language for describing his concepts, a mixture of old
myths and modern legends used to give form to some
still inconceivable realities. A flying saucer may not be
a flying saucer.

"I think it becomes almost absurd to ask whether
these other places exist in objective reality," said Puharich. "Mathematicians, for example, can create any
kind of space they want to, so long as it has logical
coherence."

The other realities may not exist within our parochial
four-dimensional world, but there also may be other
dimensions in which they can exist. A paradoxical for-

mulation: the other realities can exist only as long as they don't exist—and vice versa.

But, even granting Puharich a fruitful solipsism, he still evaded appraisal. His theory that "each individual has a small vote that can exert its small quantum of mental action on the over-all psi-plasma field"—a democratic doctrine—can be inflated into a Nietzschean apology for the Superman: he who exerts the most mental action controls reality. And *Beyond Telepathy* reveals the quiet rumblings of a dangerous elitism:

> Some people have the notion that events are predetermined, and others believe that a large element of free-will exists in man. If we take a culture which is principally a passive one, where the exertion of will power is not a prominent feature of the way of life, these people will find more evidence for determinism in their lives. This is because they are passive to the psi-plasma field around them and do not by personal intervention upset the equilibrium.
>
> On the other hand, if we take a culture where will power is a predominant feature of individual action, as for example in the long succession of Aryan [sic] cultures, we see that the psi-plasma fields are continually being influenced and changed by personal will. Such a culture will find less evidence for determinism in their affairs than will the passive cultures.

Just as individuals compete with other individuals to willfully control the future events in any given group, cultures compete with each other to willfully control the future of evolution—a theory that could easily turn ugly.

This questionable concept of evolution—a kind of transcendental universal adaptation of Erik Erikson's psychology in which specific problems must be solved within each stage of development before the individual can advance to the next highest stage—is a double seed which could grow either into a psychic fascism or into the spiritual philosophy of man's plodding evolution into god, hypothesized by Teilhard de Chardin and expanded upon by various researchers studying the nature of consciousness.

CHAPTER 16

Evolutionary Theories (1)

In MARCH, 1973, Edgar D. Mitchell, the sixth man to walk on the moon's surface, founded The Institute of Noetic Sciences, a think-tank devoted to examining human consciousness, which had its offices in Palo Alto, California, in a long two-storied building that looked like a motel. Its floors were covered with carpets the color of grass, unintentionally dramatizing one of the institute's concerns—the necessity of breaking down the conceptual barriers between what happens inside and outside, between the subjective and the objective.

" 'As above so below, as within so without'—that's from Paracelsus, the sixteenth century alchemist," said John White, the institute's director of education. "If a person has an understanding of what his personal evolution is, it seems valid to extrapolate that to the race, and from there to the universe."

After receiving his B.A. from Dartmouth College in

1961, and his M.A.T. from Yale University in 1969, White spent three years employed by the public relations department of the Southern New England Telephone Company and writing occasional free-lance articles on psychical research and altered states of consciousness. One of his projects brought him in contact with Mitchell; and in August, 1972, before Mitchell had retired from the Navy, White started working with him as writer, editor, and research associate. In August, 1973, White moved to California, as a full-time staff member of the institute, which he'd helped to form.

"One of the ways to achieve that understanding of the self," said White, "is to constantly test out the limits of your belief structure—as Blake said, to cleanse the doors of perception. What we're concerned with is a greater understanding of the nature of reality, of what this process called life is, and of to what extent the world is a projection of the self.

"Now, what is the self? We supposedly demolished the old mind-body dualism; we said, 'Well, the self is a unified organism.' Now, here we are again with spontaneous out-of-the-body experiences, spontaneous clairvoyance, and what have you. We have to ask, 'Who's in control here? Can the consciousness operate external to the body? And, if it can, is there survival of what we'll call the soul, after death?' We end up back with the old dualism in a modern idiom."

White had fallen under the same spell that had charmed Puharich. They had both become convinced that Western science had crippled its vision by focusing on man as a unified organism. Accepting the duality of man—spirit and body—was like putting on 3-D glasses; the world had more depth when you had to align two out-of-phase images.

The late twentieth century's rediscovery of spirit,

then, becomes as important for science as the development of perspective during the fifteenth century was for art. It opens up new dimensions, which previously have been impossible to represent. It gives the imagination a way of stepping back from the world and viewing the relationships among its parts, a way of getting enough distance from our reality to allow us to see what is important and what only seems important under the pressure of the moment, a way of achieving that larger view which would help us rearrange our priorities.

To get perspective White tried to blend science and myth. On the wall over his desk was a frequency spectrum chart, and he used that scientific construct as a metaphor for rationalizing out-of-the-body phenomena.

"Recorded instances of out-of-the-body experiences could possibly be placed along a spectrum of increasing densification of what used to be called the astral body or light body or solar body. In some cases, with Ingo Swann for example, his astral body is never perceived by anyone present and yet he gives a description as if he *were* physically present. In several other examples a slightly transparent astral body was perceived, not by a single percipient, but by several, all of whom saw it with changes in perspective from their physical locations. Like a hologram. In other cases, like the Landau incident which was reported in 1963 in the *Journal of the Society for Psychical Research,* the body was totally dense; you could not see through it."

In September, 1955, Eileen Landau, at her husband's request, produced an out-of-the-body experience during which she moved from one bedroom to another in what appeared to be a second body, "which was quite opaque and looked like a living person, but for the extreme pallor of the face." At one point, Landau, like Maureen Magee seeing two Melissa Stevensons at the same time, saw, near each other, both the out-of-the-body figure of his wife and his wife's physical self, which was "asleep in her bed, the bedclothes rising and falling as she breathed."

White's suggestion that all these examples of out-of-the-body experiences—the dense bodies, the translucent bodies, the bodiless consciousnesses—lay along some spectrum of out-of-the-body phenomena seemed reasonable. But even granting that, what causes the out-of-the-body body to increase or decrease its density or to vanish entirely?

Since Ingo Swann maintains complete in-body control during his out-of-the-body episodes, and his disembodied self is never seen; and since, in the two cases where an opaque disembodied self was seen, the subjects were asleep, not in control of their in-body functions, it is possible that the density of the disembodied body depends upon how much or how little the subject relinquishes control of his physical self. The more control in the in-body state, the less dense the out-of-the-body state; the less control in the in-body state, the denser the out-of-the-body state.

"It seems to me," said White, "that unless you go the route of traditional science you're not going to know very much at all; and yet going that route raises all sorts of obstacles, linguistic and otherwise. So what you have to hope for is an intuitive breakthrough which you can then test out through scientific methods—something that would seem fortuitous, but, in another sense, might happen because the universe wanted it to happen."

A universe seeking to know itself through various mobile and stationary sensors—men, animals, plants, rocks, subatomic particles, exploding stars—was one of the leitmotifs that threaded through most cosmological designs proposed by out-of-the-body researchers.

"So the universe is working through us all," said White, "and yet there is that flip-flop: in order to reach whatever goal the universe and we as part of the universe are seeking, we have to take responsibility for our own evolution at the same time that we know we are evolving the way the universe wants us to. In one sense you have to strive; in another sense you have to stop striving. It's a very complex interplay of willing and not-willing."

White carved out a universe, like one of M. C. Escher's wood-engravings in which trees grow impossible branches that become their own roots, in which an out-of-the-body experience becomes the ground upon which the in-body experience occurs and the in-body experience becomes in turn the ground for the out-of-the-body experience.

"You have to say, 'Whew, this is the way the universe wanted me to be, and I can only go along with it.' You're totally surrendering your freedom, but you're also freely choosing to make whatever decisions you must make to get where you're going. The more you surrender your freedom, the more freedom you have; the more freedom you have, the more you surrender your freedom."

White's out-of-the-body research is, to a degree, an investigation into the nature of free-will, the body becoming a Skinner box in which the soul is locked and which is regulated by a cosmic intelligence of which the soul is a part. A closed system in which the soul is both programmer and programmed. This construct untangles the problem of free-will by using Western concepts to design a Zen universe and resolves the conflict between the traditional Western impulse toward control and the contemporary reality of a society which, increasingly centralized, frustrates individual exercise of power. It is a passive philosophy that sweetens the bitterness of social impotence at the same time it invites even more centralized control.

"I personally feel that the planet is getting ready for a great leap forward," said White, sounding like a Mao of the soul. "What others have called a generation gap, I call a species gap. A new species is emerging on the planet, and all the confusion going on today is indicative of a great sifting, a great sorting out, finding out what species you belong to. Some people, I'm talking particularly about the younger people, simply have a more highly evolved nervous system. The chemicals in our food and man-made radiation are having subtle effects upon the body that are largely unaccounted for by biologists and which have had profound effects upon the mentality of the new species. But it seems necessary for one first of all to be fully grounded in the physical before there can be any real evolutionary transformation of the physical body into what occult tradition has called the solar body, the body of light."

The out-of-the-body state, according to White's paradigm, becomes evolution's preview of coming attractions, a trailer run as an earnest of what the Guiding Universal Intelligence has in store for us. We are all evolving toward disembodied beings, like caterpillars about to shuck our grosser bodies. The assumption behind his belief blends together a sixteenth-century conception of the universe in which beasts, men, and angels formed a hierarchy of being, and contemporary theories of evolution. White, mesmerized by the myth of progress, is trapped into the certainty that man's soul must be continually improved as though it were a car that every year is modified by Detroit.

"It seems to me that we have a choice," said White. "A person can deliberately take control of his own evolution and make the leap from one species to another. It may be hard; it may be painful; it may take a long time. But the choice is ours. This happening in individuals scattered throughout society would build up to a point where mankind, which is only a collection of individuals, actually would develop new psychic powers. And this would possibly be sufficient basis for transforming the race even further, a step toward building a solar body—which may take place at the level of individuals, such as you and I now exist in, but it may also take place at the level that Arthur Clarke presents in his novel *Childhood's End.*"

Clarke imagined each individual becoming part of a larger consciousness, a galactic mind, an eerie process that could be conceived as the ultimate in either cooperation or totalitarianism.

"Beyond that, galactic minds might function in a manner analogous to neurons in our brain. And galactic mind could link with galactic mind in the construction of a cosmic mind. . . ."

He sighed, as though in describing the process he suffered a painful nostalgia.

"This process of the universe becoming conscious of itself is a process a theologian might dare to describe as God."

On the first day out, coming back from the moon,

Edgar D. Mitchell stared at the earth and was filled with awe.

"It was a field-consciousness experience," said Mitchell, a term which he described in the glossary of his anthology *Psychic Exploration* as an altered state of consciousness "in which an individual seems to experience an enlargement of the ordinary boundaries of self, so that part or all of the individual's environment becomes merged with his awareness of self."

His training—a B.Sc. from Carnegie Institute of Technology in 1952; a second B.Sc. from the United States Naval Postgraduate School in 1961; a Sc.D. from the Massachusetts Institute of Technology in 1964—choked off any possible interest in psychical research until 1967, a year after he had been selected to be an astronaut. By the time he participated as the lunar-module pilot for Apollo 14 in February, 1971, he was hooked; and, during the flight between earth and moon, he engaged in a personal ESP experiment with Olaf Jonsson, a Chicago psychic, and three other people who remain unknown. The results were significantly negative; the odds against getting so few hits by chance were about 3000 to 1.

"The field-consciousness experience I had is not really close to what is called an out-of-the-body experience in that sense," said Mitchell, "so any talking you do with me will be more from a theoretical point of view—I've investigated a lot of these people, talked with a lot of them, and have formulated some tentative theories as to what we're dealing with.

"Obviously, the most simple explanation is that it is what it purports to be. Namely, there's a facet of the consciousness that is actually able to detach itself from the physiology and transport itself somewhere else. If you want to take a parsimonious view, which we tend to do, that's the explanation. Now, what that portion of consciousness is, how it relates to the rest of the so-called spirit concepts, or soul concepts, or the etheric energy of the body, the so-called auras, no one knows.

"Of course, the alternative hypothesis is that it is a form of clairvoyance in which there is nothing really traveling at all. Somehow or other, information is being gained. That is probably a bit weaker hypothesis, but it doesn't fracture modern science quite as badly as does the idea of the consciousness physically leaving the body.

"I think information can be gained both ways."

Mitchell proposed that there were three separate experiences: (1) the out-of-the-body state in which the consciousness does leave the physical; (2) the field-consciousness experience in which consciousness remains based in the body and radiates out beyond the body, like the concentric circles you make when you sink into a tub; and (3) classical clairvoyance in which you don't necessarily go anywhere at all, you just seem to have access to distant knowledge.

He furthermore made a distinction between two kinds of out-of-the-body experiences, between, for example, what Ingo Swann experiences when he claims to be out-of-his-body and what Tart's subject, Mr. X., experiences. The dissimilarity could be due to a difference in degree or in kind. In Swann's case the disembodied consciousness seemed to function as though it were a remote camera which transmitted information back to a home base—a phenomenon unlike ESP in which consciousness never separates its point or points of view from the body. In the case of Mr. X., the subject

had the sensation that the entire ego function, the perceiver and processor of information, has parted from
the flesh.

"This idea of exteriorization—which I prefer to call
it—or astral projection, or out-of-the-body experience
has been reported so often and is so much mentioned
throughout ancient literature that we mustn't discount
the possibility that it is a reality, however hard it may
be to explain."

His acceptance of the possible reality of the out-of-
the-body experience was not a deviation of a scientist-
astronaut made loony by his trip into space, but was
part of the need of Western science to pose a new
challenge once an old challenge had been met. Man
had proved he could violate outer space where he had
always placed the gods; now, he had to conquer inner
space where the gods had retreated disguised as archetypes.

Just as Robert Crookall was an occultist forced to use
the tools of rationalism in order to defend a religious
view of existence, Mitchell was a rationalist forced to
use the concepts of the occult in order to retain his
belief in the validity of Western thought, which insists
that man can accurately describe the universe and that,
having described it, can control it. To admit that there
are limits to man's mastery over his environment, both
physical and psychical, is to accept, not only a failure of
Western culture, but the end of that reasoned optimism
which has informed everything from our politics to our
art.

Mitchell's belief in the paranormal, then, is an extreme stage of Western rationalism—which, like a com-
pulsive gambler, always must raise the ante; the stakes
continually get higher and higher in a game played not

to win but for the rush that comes from the threat of losing. Once we had the means to destroy physical life on this planet, we had to find a way of risking our souls too. The danger we create goads us to find escapes; Western science amuses itself with a carrot-and-stick routine which we can never resist and which we can't afford to botch.

"The normal way we think and have been doing business is not getting us where we want to go," said Mitchell. "We are becoming more and more unstable. More and more moving surely down paths of non-survival for planetary society. We're being forced into new modes of thinking—out-of-the-body experiences or externalizations are a portion of it."

White and Mitchell discussed the out-of-the-body experience and the evolution of a new human species with corporate calm and formal lyricism, Meistersingers of a new guild of psychic craftsmen. Like Puharich and all the other consciousness researchers, they were designing new universes which, like empty houses, stood waiting for us to move in.

To make that transition, to "deliberately take control" of our own evolution, to develop the "new modes of thinking," it is necessary, however, to retrain ourselves, to reprogram our internal computers—which is what Dr. John Lilly, another member of this guild of psychics, scientists, businessmen, technologists, and former military researchers, has been learning how to do at his own consciousness-studying institute in Malibu, California.

In the early 1950s, while at the National Institute of Mental Health in Bethesda, Maryland, John Lilly began studying the effect solitude, isolation, and confinement have on consciousness. He would float in a dark, silent tank in water which was 93° Fahrenheit, blocking out as much external stimuli as possible.

In the tank, as the desire for stimulation faded, he would become aware of novel sensations: his perceiving self would feel as though it had separated from his body and was traveling into other spaces, other galaxies. Friends, acquaintances, and unusual life-forms would seem to slip into the soundless pocket he had hollowed out in his consciousness. Occasionally, he would have what appeared to be paranormal experiences, episodes of ESP. But the Korean War had sensitized the government to the possibilities of brainwashing; the government began exploiting Lilly's research for purposes he disapproved of; and, in 1958, Lilly left the National Institute of Mental Health to set up a project in the Virgin Islands whose aim was to study dolphin intelligence.

Lilly, who was born on January 6, 1915, received his B.A. from the California Institute of Technology in Pasadena and his M.D. from the University of Pennsylvania. Before joining the National Institute of Mental Health in 1953, he did post-doctoral work in bio- and neurophysics and he trained at the Philadelphia Association for Psychoanalysis.

During the twelve years he spent in dolphin research, he continued to engage in his solitude, isolation, and confinement experiments; and in the early 1960s he used LSD as part of his tank studies. In all this work those other life-forms he had discovered continued to haunt him—or perhaps he continued to haunt them. In "Inner Space and Parapsychology," a paper which was published in the *Proceedings of the Parapsychological Association* (Number 6, 1969), Lilly said:

There were entities that could think straight into me and I would think straight into them. There were entities that appeared with no palpable external realities as we know it—centers of light is one image that one can use, but actually they were centers of feeling, cognition, and all the rest of it. Then there are the others that are described in the Bardos and the Eastern literature, some of which I didn't like at all and apparently they didn't like me.

After leaving dolphin research, convinced that he had communicated with dolphins and no longer wanting to experiment on creatures whose brains were larger than man's (and who were possibly more intelligent), Lilly strolled through the twentieth century's flourishing gnostic underworld—the Esalen Institute at Big Sur, California; Oscar Ichazo's streamlined Sufi cult in Chile—following his only dogma: "What one believes to be true either *is* true, or *becomes* true in one's mind, within limits to be determined experimentally or experientially. *These limits are beliefs to be transcended.*"

Like Blue Harary, Lilly created a universe out of his imagination; but, unlike Blue, he was not comfortable inhabiting the world he created, too aware that it was a temporary construct. He treated out-of-the-body research as a probe for the first cause, continually disassembling his world, hoping to discover what Jung called "objective cognition," which, if it is the first cause, becomes equal to God.

Shortly after returning from Chile, Lilly established his institute, Human Software, Inc.; and, like the hermits who used to retreat into the desert, he retreated into his isolation tank, surfacing to communicate with the outer world cryptically, in scientific parables. The seductive visions of Puharich, Mitchell, and White became, in Lilly's work, baroque systems welded together like wrought iron gates that barred the way into his universe.

He began with a metaphor, common enough in science fiction magazines like *Analog* and *If:* Man is a human biocomputer, and to survive we must learn how to replace our destructive programs with constructive programs. This can be done by creating new metaprograms, which are the large systems that control the smaller systems.

Different metaprograms are associated with different levels of consciousness—an ego metaprogram with an ego-oriented level of consciousness, a cosmic metaprogram with a cosmic level of consciousness. To change a metaprogram one must go to the appropriate level— like stopping an elevator on the right floor. In *The Center Of The Cyclone*, an autobiographical account of his pilgrimage, which was published in 1972, Lilly located nine levels of consciousness that corresponded to the vibrational levels identified by George Ivanovitch Gurdjieff, a Greek mystic who died in 1949.

Level Plus-Minus 48 is the neutral condition on earth, "the state . . . for the reception and transmission of new data." Plus-24 "is the level for creative thought," in which one operates when absorbed in a pleasant task. In Plus-12 "one is in the body . . . but not doing a job on the planetside trip." It is the state of religious bliss. Plus-6 "is that state in which one focuses one's consciousness down to a very small point," the out-of-the-body condition. The roar Claudette Kiely reported hearing as she shot out of her body occurs, according to Lilly, when one is moving from level Plus-12 into level Plus-6. Plus-3 is "fusion with universal mind," transcendence. The other four states are negative versions of these Plus-states. For example, in Minus-3 one merges with all the evil in the universe; it is "the deepest hell of which one can conceive."

"The tendency is to assume that the various levels of consciousness all are simulations of space within the central nervous system," said Lilly. "You're exploring your own unconscious. However, as you penetrate deeper, you come up against the unknown, and new things start happening that can't be accounted for by anything in your own history."

Lilly explained that there were three hypotheses which might resolve that conflict: (1) Man's "computer simulation system" may be more flexible than we would assume, creating situations that are new, but still synthetic. (2) "The new things" that start happening when one penetrates the unknown may actually *be* new experiences which become available because one really does, in some sense, leave the physical body. And (3) "you stay inside your nervous system, but you open up channels of communication and control into other dimensions in which some sort of intelligence—either a non-human cosmic consciousness or a civilization far advanced beyond ours—is operating. In other words, you get into a feedback relationship with far-out civilizations. If they know as much more than we do as we know than we knew in 1890, say, only eighty years ago, this is perfectly feasible."

Perfectly feasible. Whatever could be imagined became perfectly feasible in that mazy world my search had led me to: inside became outside, mind became substance, imagination's quirks became signals from far-out civilizations. When I talked with Lilly, his suggestion did not seem quite mad, as it would have half a year before. It was merely a very improbable theory to be considered along with the other improbable theories I had been collecting—weird concepts which I found threatening.

Whatever other realities there were, I enjoyed what Lilly called "the planetside trip," and to accept these other visions would be to damn myself to a world which would fade in and out like a poor television picture. The chair I was sinking into could dissolve, transforming itself into a cosmic rocker, swaying back and forth across the Milky Way. I wanted to be able to drink untranscendental glasses of water.

Lilly explained that the secret to not losing your sense of the reality of the planetside trip was to employ the magic *as if* which Method actors were taught to use while creating stage realities. In an out-of-the-body experience, you program your biocomputer to perceive *as if* your consciousness were separated from your body.

"You map within the computer a position three feet above your head," said Lilly, "and program your observing-I to view the world *as if* it were up there."

Using the *as if* avoids the problem of trying to decide whether or not an out-of-the-body episode really occurs —which may, in fact, be an unsolvable question, because, as Puharich said, "it becomes almost absurd to ask whether these other places exist in objective reality."

"When you are in these far-out states, these nonordinary states, they are real," said Lilly. "You believe they are real. You accept them as real. And this planet, this reality do not exist.

"Then, you are forced back to this planet and this reality somehow. You get squeezed back into this vehicle, your body; and you look in the glove compartment, read the instructions on how to run the vehicle, and suddenly you realize you're re-identifying with the self-metaprogrammer in that biocomputer."

Just as you experienced the far-out spaces *as if* they were real, you experience this world *as if* it were real once you return to your body. The old riddle of Chuang-tzu: Is the dream dreaming the dreamer?

Both the far-out spaces and our familiar world are only models of possible realities, "limits . . . to be transcended." But man, according to Lilly, is a naive psychic traveler; and like the yokel who goes to a Kansas City strip show in Rodgers and Hammerstein's *Oklahoma!*, he keeps thinking that the cosmos, shedding one layer of illusion after another, has gone about as far as it can go.

"Once in a while," said Lilly, "I'll come back from one of these spaces and say, 'Baby-dolls, this is the truth with a capital *T.*' For example, the other day, coming out of the tank, I'd arrived at a point at which I said, 'The cosmic computer created us to keep itself informed about the local microcosm. Our physical bodies are just part of the Network. The local part, that's all. And there are some people who are more consciously hooked in to Network than others.'

"But I learned a long time ago to be suspicious of the feeling of being sure you've hit the truth. Awe, reverence, hyper-enthusiasm are states of consciousness, not evidence that what you're experiencing is true."

Every time Lilly described a useful fiction about the universe, he disowned it, as though he were suffering from a bad conscience, knowing that words could never communicate what he had undergone. But, despite his disclaimers, he tried to give the impression he knew more than he told and believed more than he knew. Most out-of-the-body experiences, he said, occur on Plus-6, because on Plus-6 you still have an identity.

"On Plus-3, you have no identity. Once you've been to Plus-3, you begin to lose the pride in the vehicle— the hubris that's connected with that. That's the most dangerous thing the human being has: A belief in his own identity."

Believing too much in one's identity prevents one from experiencing a union with all being, Lilly suggested; and this illusion of identity leads people into taking seriously all the ego-games and conflicts which drain their energies away from the truly serious business of spiritual development.

According to Lilly, the consciousness that separates from the body during an exteriorization is not the same one that comes back.

"Every time a consciousness leaves the body," he said, "somebody else comes back. They just take on the programming that the other one put in there, and the one before him and the one before him. You can change connectors every night. That wouldn't make any difference."

Lilly's absurd idea evokes echoes of Jerome S. Bruner's speculations on the preprogrammed infant mind. All knowledge is already there when the child is born, ready to become usable once the proper stimulus is applied, only instead of coming and going every night, consciousness would come and stay with the body until death. Bruner's serious thoughts on the way children learn help to make Lilly's ideas more accessible, but they do not make them any less bizarre.

"Another way of saying this," Lilly continued, "is that an extraterrestrial agent takes over for twenty-four hours to get trained. See what I mean? Then, when the body goes to sleep, it leaves and another one takes over for *his* training trip the next day. A continuous rotation through the vehicle. All paranormal phenomena in our reality is just this Network working through our bodies. This happened to me several times. I got out of the way and allowed the Network to use me. And boy, they'll use you!"

Lilly's Network, an intergalactic energy Mafia, is another version of Puharich's cosmic evolution and White's universal mind—senseless inventions to make sense out of creation. Since both science and religion have failed to piece together any coherent, secure belief-system in the twentieth century, all these desperate rationalists have married the two mythologies hoping that the old and barren can, like Abraham and Sarah, miraculously produce. The alternative is grisly.

The parallels which science fiction enthusiasts like to draw between the fire that destroyed Sodom and Gomorrah after Abraham and Sarah left and the nuclear holocaust that could destroy mankind is apt—not as history, but as parable. If we cannot conceive a new ethic, then we will go up in flames; and there won't be any Isaac left to seed a civilization to replace the lost old one. Belief in the out-of-the-body experience, whether or not the experience itself is real, is one expression of this urge toward a new ethic. But a new ethic based upon the kind of trust in Greater Powers implied in Puharich's and Lilly's visions could lead to a rigid society that demands blind obedience to an elite which claims to mediate between those Greater Powers and the ruck of mankind.

CHAPTER 17

Evolutionary Theories (2)

WHITE SUGGESTED that humans, their out-of-the-body consciousnesses joined, might someday become god-like; Lilly suggested that out-of-the-body godlike intelligences already exist in the universe; and Robert Monroe, a former radio and television producer, combined aspects of both of these odd theories to suggest that some humans have already in the out-of-the-body state met godlike intelligences on their own celestial turf and are halfway to godhood themselves.

On a fall evening in 1958, Monroe, then forty-three years old, stretched out on his bed with his arm hanging over the edge of the mattress and pushed his fingertips through the floor. He shoved his hand deeper and felt in the space between his floorboards and the ceiling of the room below a woodchip, a nail, sawdust. . . . The strange feeling that his body was vibrating, which had

held his consciousness suspended like a feather in an
updraft, began to vanish; and, not knowing what had
happened, afraid his arm might be trapped in the wood
if he left it stuck through the floor when the vibrations
ended, he yanked up his hand.

He had recently left a vice-presidency at the Mutual
Broadcasting System in New York City and had bought
his own radio station, WAAA in Winston-Salem, North
Carolina; and he could not afford to waste time in what
he at first assumed were occult fantasies.

But the fantasies refused to vanish. He would be lying
on his bed or on his office couch, the vibrations would
begin to prickle along his body, and suddenly he would
slip from his flesh as easily as a slick sliver of soap can
slide through wet fingers. He would find himself floating on the ceiling, staring down at his physical body
resting peacefully in bed. Or he would find himself
flying through space, a specter Superman, to homes of
friends or to other more exotic, sometimes sinister
spots: the edge of the universe, a parallel world, or a
Busby Berkeley version of heaven, full of awe-inspiring
processions of inconceivable powers.

He considered committing himself to an asylum, but
despite an occasional out-of-the-body flight he was
functioning well in his normal, waking life. So, accepting the experience as a harmless excursion into an altered state of consciousness, he decided to try a few
domestic experiments to determine how much of the
experience was real and how much was fantasy.

He extended his consciousness to locations around his
office and his home and later tried to verify if what he
had perceived had actually happened at the time he
was projecting. Once, while out of his body, he visited
a skeptical friend, and, to prove he had been there, he

pinched her. A few days later when he asked her if she'd been molested by any ghostly hands over the weekend, he claimed she pulled up her sweater and showed him two black and blue marks—an indication that not only had he really been present at a distant spot in some disembodied form, but that his disembodied self could inexplicably interact with the physical world.

The evidence that the experience was in large measure real fascinated him, both because of its serious implications and because of its frivolous, even lewd, possibilities. Monroe was the only out-of-the-body adept who admitted to being charmed by the opportunities for mischief that the out-of-the-body experience offered. Although he resisted the pubescent dream of strolling invisible through the girls' high school locker room, he did concede that he had erotic impulses and on one occasion accepted the invitation to sample out-of-the-body sex—albeit with out-of-the-body creatures. Like Blue, Monroe claimed to have encountered bodiless and partially-bodied intelligences when he was in the out-of-the-body state. He said he stumbled across a group of these out-of-the-body men and women in September, 1963. When they perceived Monroe, they formed a row; and, as he walked from one to the other, they each stepped forward and zapped him with sex—sort of like bopping through one of those late 1950s line dances. Monroe described the sex as being a frictionless flash like a blue electric spark snapping between two short-circuiting wires.

Although Monroe felt fairly sure that the out-of-the-body experience was real, he knew that his private experiments could never be conclusive; so, when he met Charles Tart in 1965, he agreed to participate in the series of experiments which Tart later wrote up, calling Monroe Mr. X.

Because of his autobiographical book, *Journeys Out Of The Body,* Monroe is well-known. Although his book is a lineal descendant of the occult accounts of Yram, Fox, and Muldoon, he is generally respected among serious parapsychologists, as though his success as a businessman and his reputation as a sober citizen were negotiable assets, readily transformed into a protective aura of trustworthiness.

"I grew up in Lexington, Kentucky," said Monroe, "and I had a very happy childhood."

Monroe, tall and slightly overweight, had the canny squint and the artlessly cynical smile of a small carnival owner or of LBJ in a David Levine caricature. He shambled around the five houses already plunked down on the bulldozed red dirt of "Green Meadow," a projected 116-home community, one of three suburban developments being built near Charlottesville, Virginia, by his construction company, Process Builders Corporation. He did not look like a man who had been sliding in and out of his body for the past fifteen years, mapping the psychic universe he had discovered in his out-of-the-body state. He had not cultivated any mysterious mannerisms. He dressed, not in black capes, but in baggy slacks, wrinkled shirt, and wilted sports coat.

"When I decided to move south to Charlottesville from New York in 1961," he said, "I drew a line along a parallel with Lexington, so I could be in a place that had the same climate as my childhood home. My mother was an M.D. in Lexington, and my father was a professor of Romance languages at a college there. Transylvania College." Which, delightfully enough, really exists.

More than any of the other out-of-the-body adepts, Monroe has fun with the phenomenon, both during and after his experiences. He enjoyed presenting himself to me as a bit sinister. He was slyly aware of his position in a society that distrusted the paranormal, and he liked to set up and deflate my skepticism.

"I'm a Scorpio, born in 1915," he said, "not that I'm a follower of astrology. My father became a professor at Ohio State, so my family moved to Columbus, Ohio, in 1930, when I was in high school. If I've had any traumatic shock in my life, it was moving from a pleasant small Southern town to a large, cold Northern city."

After receiving a B.A. from Ohio State, Monroe started a summer theater in western Pennsylvania. But the theater closed after a month, and Monroe took a job at a radio station in Cleveland, then moved to another in Cincinnati in 1938. Convinced that he had directing and writing talent, he wrote, asking for a job, to a nutritionist in New York City who had a radio program. Thinking a friendly return letter was an offer, Monroe left for New York. He went to the nutritionist's office, and announced he was ready to work.

The nutritionist, embarrassed that some kid had come all the way from Ohio on the vague possibility of a job, gave Monroe some free-lance scripts to do. A year and a half later, around 1940, NBC bought his radio show "Rocky Gordon," a story about railroading, which was slated five days a week. From "Rocky Gordon," Monroe moved into advertising, and from advertising he moved into his own production company, which by 1950 was turning out about twelve network shows each day—quiz shows, comedy shows, dramatic shows.

"But it was an unreal thing," said Monroe, "this life-drama in the studio. One of the things that turned me away from production and directing was my feeling that this was a non-reality and that reality was taking place outside that studio somewhere."

So in the late 1950s, about the same time he started having his first out-of-the-body episodes, he left producing. By slipping from his body, Monroe felt that he was not withdrawing from reality but cracking through the material shell into a greater reality, the same transcendental outback that Zen masters and saints explored. Leaving the body became for Monroe, not just an unusual state of awareness to be explored in and out of a laboratory, but a tool, a way of escaping the limitations of the flesh.

"In your early separation from your physical body," he said, "you retain the memory of your humanoid form. It's like a mold that you've been in, but the more you become aware of this as a plastic unit, the more you take other forms. I could become a dog. It may not be a perfect dog, but I'd get the eyes in the right place and the teeth long enough. Perhaps this is where the idea of the werewolf came from. These days I don't think I normally have any arms or legs when I am apart from the physical body. I think I am a blob of some kind. Or a teardrop. Or a ball."

His description of his limbless disembodied self evoked the image of the great hokum head with which the Wizard of Oz fooled Dorothy, and there was a slight Barnum air about Monroe. He was a crafty businessman with a quick eye for a ripe opportunity. While driving home to his 640-acre estate, Whistlefield Farm, he free-associated money-making schemes.

"If someone offered to mow that grass on the median strip free for the state," he said, "he could make a hell of a lot of money selling the hay."

He juggled the material and spiritual worlds neatly, playing alternately two contradictory roles: the worldly businessman and the psychic adventurer. His conversation glided from making hay to the technique of walking through walls, as though he did not see any great distinction between the two realities. They were equally humdrum, equally exciting.

He used the salesman's and storyteller's tricks of pausing in the middle of a phrase for suspense and of sliding the end of one sentence into the beginning of another to keep the listener hooked. He was such an interesting conversationalist that even his cats enjoyed talking to him.

"Hello, cat," Monroe said as he eased himself into a chair on the screened-in porch of his house at Whistlefield Farm.

"Maeow," said the cat.

"How are you?" Monroe asked.

"Maeow," said the cat.

"Catch any mice today?" Monroe asked.

"Maeow," said the cat.

"The cat just always talks to him," said Scooter, one of Monroe's daughters.

"One of the most remarkable things that happened recently," Monroe said, "was encountering an animal intelligence. It was a pathetic little thing. I just rolled out of the body, and I encountered this life form. I thought, *Well, I'll make an inquiry of it,* meaning I'll try to perceive it. And this little life form was just radiating love. I thought, *What is this?* This radiation came back just as clear as anything, 'The only way I can show my love is by licking you.' Then I felt on my arm *lick, lick, lick, lick,* like this. I said, 'That's enough; I understand.' And I rolled back into the body, sat up, and looked around. Here was one of these Siamese cats, looking at me with the funniest look. Coincidence? Reality? I don't know."

I asked him why he thought he had begun having the experiences—not just what had triggered them, but what had allowed them to be triggered in the first place.

"I never had any interest in this type of thing before," he said. "It was totally new and quite alien. I was just a businessman, minding my own business. No psychic experiences when I was a child.

"Not too long before the first experience, I did have some teeth recapped, and I've sometimes wondered whether the application of any metals in the capping may have influenced some electrolyte activity inside my mouth, which may have in some way led to the experiences. But that's just a stab in the dark.

"I was also doing some experiments with a tape recorder and sleep-learning which may have had something to do with it, although I have no idea how. I talked about that in my book. And it has been suggested that the fumes I inhaled from some wood glue I was using to build some cupboards about that time may have had some effect. But I'm not sure.

"I just don't think I'm that special. I just think that I'm the one who was looking the other way and fell into the manhole. Everybody else was walking around it."

On a hill overlooking the horse pasture and the bass pond at Whistlefield Farm, Monroe has built an institute for the study of out-of-the-body experiences, an administration building with two offices, a lounge, and a library, which is connected to a laboratory wing with three isolation chambers, a control center, and a large test room.

"We're getting our instrumentation in soon—electro-encephalographs, polygraphs, all sorts of machinery," said Monroe.

He waved at a door which, as though mimicking the psychic threshold leading to the out-of-the-body state, opened onto nothing, no step, a three-foot drop.

"We put that door in so we can expand," he said.

Next to the administration-laboratory building was a guest house, intended for those who will help Monroe chart the three distinct out-of-the-body worlds he claims to have discovered. The first world, the *Here-Now*, exists in our material universe during the time of the experience; it is our ordinary reality, which, when he is in his out-of-the-body state, bores Monroe. The only problem in sailing around the *Here-Now* is getting used to passing through familiar walls and flying thirty or forty feet above the earth.

"There really isn't much to do in the *Here-Now*," said Monroe. "Let's say, if this morning at three you rolled out of your body, what would you do? Visit your wife? And after you had done that twenty times and it was commonplace, what would you do?"

Infinity, Eternity, the second out-of-the-body locale, is a non-material world whose laws correspond only vaguely to the laws of our material world, it looks like something staged by both Stanley Kubrick and Dante. In *Infinity, Eternity* one can wander off to ride Saturn's rings as though they were some cosmic merry-go-round, swim through an infernal sea of sucker-like creatures, or drop in on one of the local heavens, where the out-of-the-body crowd drift around in white gowns and fall on their backs to make a living road for some great, unidentified, but infinitely powerful, presence. Time and space don't exist.

"Locale 2," Monroe said, "as far as I can see, has no ending. There must be an infinite variety of dimensions. It takes some guts to do them. Some of them are most disconcerting, but they're there."

The third out-of-the-body locale is the *Reverse Image*, a world reminiscent of Vladimir Nabokov's anti-terra in *Ada*. It is either a mirrored version of our familiar universe, a parallel world, a stepsister earth, or a terrestrial society in the far past or the far future.

"Atomic power was commonplace," Monroe said, "but electricity was not."

In the *Reverse Image* the cars are larger and are steered by a horizontal bar and the roads are double the width of our highways. Monroe avoided Locale 3, because whenever he has visited it he has found himself projected into the body of a fellow who was not having a very pleasant time.

Like the creatures that populate Blue Harary's out-of-the-body space, Monroe's out-of-the-body beings are usually shadowy things at the edge of sight, flitting through his world unannounced and anonymous, although once two of the beings climbed onto his disembodied back and wouldn't get off. When he pulled, they stretched like rubber. Terrified, he struggled with them like Jacob wrestling with the Angel; finally, tearing them off, he held one in each hand, stymied until another out-of-the-body being, a man in a dark robe, appeared and took them away, one nestled in each arm.

Monroe explained that these Helpers have often aided him at crucial moments.

"About three years ago," he said, "a blockage developed in the carotid arteries between the heart and the brain. They had to put this tube in and bypass the blockage. They can open up the arteries, take a rotorooter, and clear it out. I warned the anesthetist, 'Look, I throw these things off very fast.' He nodded, 'Yes, yes, I'll put you down real strong.' Well, I came back to full consciousness, lying on the operating table; and they were sewing up these slits in the neck . . ."

He described his body from a distance—"the heart, the brain, the neck"—as though it were merely the old Miller engine he tinkered with when he was a kid.

". . . I opened one eye," Monroe continued, "and I said, 'Oh, no. Get me back where I was. Hey, please, give me something to get rid of this horrible pain.' People ask me, 'Well, why didn't you simply get away from the pain by rolling out of the body?' I thought of it, but I got a great message: 'Don't do it, kid. It's so hard coming back, you won't make it.'

"All these assistants have one thing in common. Without exception they treat me as someone who is a very dear friend who can't remember who he is. It's like that old Hindu story—you may remember it— where the prince left India to go to Egypt in search of some kind of fantastic jewel. And he got so preoccupied with the search that he forgot he was a prince of India. And somebody had to go to remind him what he was."

Helpers, disembodied people, disembodied cats. . . . The psychic space at Whistlefield Farm sounded as though it were as crowded as Central Park on a sunny Sunday afternoon. Even Monroe's editor, Bill Whitehead, was disturbed by a vagrant apparition when he visited the farm.

"I had an extraordinary weekend," Whitehead had told me over the telephone a few days before I flew— in my body and in an airplane—down to Charlottesville. "Bob asked me how I'd slept, and I said, 'There was a dull light in the middle of the room . . . like a fluorescent light coming from a distance and casting a glow. I had an impulse to get up and move, go somewhere else. I fought it. Went back to sleep.' The next morning Bob said, 'I don't want to alarm you since you have another night here.' Later, he told me that the light was a kind of being, another person or thing, that seems to be hanging around the house recently."

When speculating about the meaning of his out-of-the-body experiences, Monroe punctuated his statements with frequent long sighs, because he knew that the only way he could describe what he thought was happening to him was with outrageous fables. In a chapter he decided not to include in his book, he explained that our purpose on earth is to produce emotional energy—what he called *loosh,* a term he invented because it would have no associations—which is food for the gods.

"We are like Guernseys," he said. "Gods' cows. Now, suppose a cow attempted to communicate with the farmer? It would arouse the farmer's curiosity about this unusual animal. The people who try to communicate with the god-farmers, who are no longer Guernseys, are the messiahs and sages and saviors of history. Surprisingly, there are some people on earth now who are no longer Guernseys. I found this out much to my surprise from some very well-known research psychologists with fairly significant reputations for integrity. I can't tell you who they are because I was given it on a very confidential level. But wouldn't that rather surprise you?"

It was tempting to dismiss Monroe's fables as benign ravings or excellent, although derivative, science fiction. His descriptions of his out-of-the-body flights, more theatrical than the descriptions of most of the other adepts I met, sounded a little like the art of *jaunt-ing* in Alfred Bester's novel *The Demolished Man,* and his theories about *loosh* seemed a tepid brew of Gurd-jieff's mysticism.

And I was disturbed by some hints of invention in Monroe's stories. In his book he told of meeting an out-of-the-body being who was dressed in a monk's robe and who told him, "You were last a monk in Co-shocton, Pennsylvania."

"Recently," Monroe wrote, "a Catholic priest friend took the trouble to investigate this possibility of past-life monasticism. To my surprise and delight, there is an obscure monastery near Coshocton."

Coshocton, Pennsylvania, however, does not exist. There is a Capuchin order about thirty-five miles from Coshocton, *Ohio,* which is curiously not too far from Columbus where Monroe grew up; and there is an Augustinian order at Villanova University, which, al-though not particularly obscure, is about a ten-minute drive from a Pennsylvania town called Conshohocken.

"I couldn't find Coshocton, Pennsylvania, on the map either," said Monroe, not at all rattled by the discrep-ancy. "Since I've never heard of Conshohocken, in the out-of-body state I must have heard it as Coshocton."

That failed to explain how he could claim a friendly priest confirmed the monastery near Coshocton, Penn-sylvania. But Monroe shrugged off inaccuracies in his book as easily as he avoided specific dates and names in conversation. Inconsistencies were insignificant. The first maps of the Americas may not have been accurate, but they did stick continents on the other side of the Atlantic Ocean—and, of course, early explorers did re-turn with tall tales.

Osis may have been correct when he described most

people with psi-abilities as being "flighty" with facts; and the various disembodied beings and other dimensions could be indications, not that the out-of-the-body experience is merely a dream, but that, as Tart had suggested, it may be a dream mixed with "something else."

Taking that cue from Tart, I asked Monroe how he knew most of his experiences were not just fantasies. What proof did he have they were real?

"I haven't been looking for proof," he said, escaping my question like an illusionist dropping through a trap door in the floor of a stage. "I satisfied myself, and that's all I need to do. I've gone on to something else. In recent years, I've been attending what I loosely define as a class. We went above the earth and began to elate, to get bigger. Don't ask me what the technique of this was. We got to one point where we could stand off here, and the earth was a ball about two feet in diameter. You could put your hands out on both sides of it this way or reach over and touch the moon on the other side. You understand what we were being taught? Gradually we were taught to get the moon and the earth so they would fit in the palm of your hand. I'm symbolizing 'hand,' but basically this is what it was. We learned to elate more broadly. We could put our arms around the whole solar system this way."

Monroe heaved himself up from the couch on the dark porch of his house. Behind him in the night fields, fireflies sparkled like synapses in a giant brain. Monroe stretched and said:

"It's all a matter of perspective."

PART 4

CONCLUSION

Trusting and credulous as I am, it is normal for me to be continually on my guard and not to read a supernatural significance into events too quickly.

JEAN COCTEAU, *Opium*

CHAPTER 18

The Real And The True

BLUE HARARY DESCRIBED being in the out-of-the-body state as inhabiting a thought. Anything becomes possible because nothing is real. John Lilly, similarly characterizing the phenomenon, also stressed the primacy of imagination in creating the reality within which the out-of-the-body experience exists. Both of them wavered in their explanations of whether or not there was some seed of objective reality around which the subjective realities could crystallize. At various times both confirmed that they believed there was; at other times they would deny it. The solution to this contradiction lies in the paradox that, if there is an objective reality, it is inaccessible to normal human understanding. It can only be approached through a transformed consciousness; and the transformation of consciousness, the act itself, may somehow be both the ground upon which

that objective reality operates and the boundary between the world created by the imagination and the
objective world which the imagination uses to build
upon. In practice, the interplay between the objective
and subjective realities would become a subtle negotia-
tion.

"You are moving slowly in your second-state body,"
Robert Monroe said, "and you go to this wall. It seems
like the wall has the same kind of surface tension we
might find in a cup of water. You push against it, then
you pass through it easily. When you move rapidly, you
break this quickly. You don't even notice it. As often
happens in my case now, I'll roll out of the physical; and
I vaguely feel myself floating down through the bed,
down through the floor. But it's not an atom-by-atom or
a layer-by-layer feeling."

According to this theory, if the material world exists
in an objective condition, it exists as a protean physical
reality which can be molded by imagination. Monroe in
his out-of-the-body state floated up to the wall, met
resistance, and, instead of eliminating the wall (which
he could not do if there is some objective physical reality), he may have merely redefined the concept of the
wall so it would allow his consciousness to pass through.
If the theory is obscure, it is because the concepts resist
expression; but it is useful to entertain such arcane
speculation, because, if the out-of-the-body phenomenon is authentic—and that is, of course, still a moot
point—it may be necessary, as Blue and many of the
other researchers and adepts have suggested, to rede-
sign our conception of reality.

Without straying from our traditional assumptions
about reality, however, it seems safe to claim that the
sensation of consciousness separating from the flesh can

be induced by certain specific and ordinary procedures which operate within our everyday world.

"Just sit down," said Ingo Swann, "and concentrate on a target someplace. I used to run a little test for myself. I'd say, 'Well, I have to go to the subway now, so I'll go down and try and see what's in the store windows, before I get to it.' It's just a matter of assuming it can be done without making a great fuss about it."

Monroe's recipe for leaving the body, although akin to Swann's, is less active. Like Blue and Claudette Kiely, he counsels the novice: lie down, count mentally from one to twenty, breathing deeply with each number and conditioning yourself to become more relaxed with each breath. Your skin may start tingling around number seven; and, if you are lucky and haven't fallen asleep by number twenty, you may be seized with violent trembling. When you spring up, wondering what happened, you may, on glancing over your shoulder to make sure you haven't stretched out on a live electric wire, discover your physical body lying peacefully where you left it.

Once your spirit is soaring, Monroe claimed, there was no danger of misplacing your body like losing a car you parked in a multilevel garage.

"Returning?" he said. "It's as though you have to sneeze, but it's not your nose tickling."

Although all these methods seem to involve the same sort of steps that could lead to self-hypnosis, out-of-the-body adepts deny that the experience is due to autosuggestion.

"The experience is hard to describe," said Andrija Puharich, "but it's certainly not a trance. It's like intense concentration. The essence of it is learning how to switch the body onto automatic pilot. You switch the heart system, the brain system, the respiratory system, all those systems that keep you from getting out of your body, onto automatic pilot, and you're free. The body's on its own, and you go off on a trip."

No one has conclusively proved that the out-of-the-body experience is not some sort of trance, but there is evidence that the state is distinct from certain trance-like conditions—for example, it is, according to Morris's experimental data, different from what Blue called his "cooling-off period." Also, despite the fact that some similarities exist between sensations experienced during out-of-the-body episodes and those experienced during vivid dreaming, those two phenomena appear to be unrelated. Brain wave activity associated with the two states is often quite different. Charles Tart's first subject had her out-of-the-body episodes "in conjunction with a non-dreaming, non-awake brain-wave stage characterized by predominant slowed alpha activity from her brain and no activation of the autonomic nervous system," and his second subject, Robert Monroe, did not produce the delta waves which one generally sees "within half an hour of falling asleep in all subjects." The brain-wave patterns which both Ingo Swann and Blue Harary exhibited during their out-of-the-body states were also not typical of dreaming.

Although out-of-the-body experiences are not necessarily either trances or dreaming, most of the episodes do seem to occur during states of deep relaxation. Poynton's study in South Africa, in which he discovered that seventy-six per cent of those who responded to his survey had the sensations of consciousness separating from the body while they were physically relaxed, is supported by Celia Green's findings that people had out-of-the-body experiences when they were lying down three times more frequently than when they were sitting. As soon as Krippner's subject became anxious about the experiment, realizing that he was on the edge of having an out-of-the-body experience, the experience eluded him. Kiely and Tanous, like Monroe, prime themselves for the experience by relaxing. Melissa, Puharich, and Tart's first subject all had their episodes of feeling themselves out of their bodies while they were asleep. And, even when the subjects' out-of-the-body experiences were precipitated by crises, the tension involved in responding to the crisis was usually followed by a sudden relaxation—as in Bob Hall's case, when the terror of falling 3400 feet gave way to an acceptance of the disaster.

Most of the conditions that can induce the out-of-the-body experience seem to involve this typical movement from a state of greater to one of lesser excitement. Dick French tended to have his feelings of being out of the body when he lay down to rest after doing exhausting physical work. Tom Blackwell's experience occurred during a release of sexual energy. This tends to support both Noyes's psychological theory that such experiences happen when there is a sudden redirection of psychic energy and Puharich's physiological theory that they are a result of an interplay of cholinergia and adrenergia.

Furthermore, this movement from a state of greater to lesser excitement, this abrupt redirection of psychic energy, may cause a temporary disorientation in a subject, which could contribute to conditions conducive of out-of-the-body experiences. There does seem to be evidence to support such speculation. Palmer's star subject, confused by the noise and the lights in the experimental environment, found himself confronting a mental image of himself—an apparition of his own body—which then became the locus of his consciousness. By unconsciously objectifying himself in this way, he became open to accepting any apparent reality which would account for his feelings of dissociation.

Other experiences of sensory overload—like Rosalind Heywood's overwhelming realization of how beautiful the rose bushes were or Doug Fauntleroy's intense concentration on the pattern made by the traffic lights—could function just as effectively in triggering out-of-the-body experiences as Palmer's experiment had. And the conditions of sensory deprivation which Lilly used to spark his out-of-the-body episodes probably work in a similar way. The disorientation which results from blocking off sensory reference points prompts the subject to construct temporary reference points which mimic those usually given by the senses; and, since consciousness then begins operating in relation to those temporary points of reference, it feels, perhaps is, freed of the body, which it then objectifies.

But physical or psychophysiological triggers cannot be made to account entirely for the out-of-the-body experience. The type of personality most susceptible to such episodes also has to be considered, particularly those predisposed to psychic experiences in the first place. Kiely, Tanous, Rogo, Heywood, and Puharich were all involved in the paranormal before they had their first out-of-the-body sensations. They accepted the phenomenon as possible, and perhaps this openness helped to induce their experiences.

A willing acceptance of the paranormal, however, can be only one of a number of factors contributing to a susceptibility to the out-of-the-body experience. A sense of alienation, certainly, seems to be another element in the personalities of those who are susceptible to the episodes. Janice Carduner's abrupt objectification of herself—"I'm married to a person who wears glasses"—could lead her to create a mental image of herself as someone other, someone who is defined not by a subjective response to the world but by a specific external fact.

Perhaps an even more significant component in the personalities of those susceptible to such experiences might be, as Freud suggested, a need to compensate for certain unsatisfying aspects of reality. Such a need could be the result of a temporary discontent, like Doug Fauntleroy's dissatisfaction at having to drop out of school to work in an automobile factory or Rosalind Heywood's momentary unsated sexual desire. Or it could stem from a more deep-seated cause, such as Blue's friendless childhood or whatever in Tanous's background prompted him to claim a degree he did not yet have. Or a need to compensate may be an expression of a lingering but not necessarily deep-seated disappointment—which may be what touches off out-of-the-body experiences in people like Robert Monroe, who, having started out as a writer, appears to use his paranormal episodes as counterweights against the businessman he has become.

When one focuses on what is lacking in life, it is hard not to depersonalize the self: I am someone who is lonely; I am someone who is frustrated. . . . The more someone is unhappy with his world, the more likely it is that he will attempt to recreate that world, changing it to make it more acceptable, and the more open he will be to any description of existence that would give him control over reality. For this reason, many people attracted to the out-of-the-body phenomenon—both those who experience the sensations and those who study the subject—rationalize the unknown by creating philosophies which place emphasis on the individual's power to change the world through an act of mind, to (as Blue said) "think things into existence."

By thinking things into existence, someone can furnish the empty places in a life. The feeling of having an out-of-the-body self which has powers the in-body self lacks, and the belief in a world which the out-of-the-body self inhabits, satisfy the unfulfilled needs of the susceptible personality and fill the psychic void.

Throughout my study of the out-of-the-body phenomenon, I tried to avoid asking questions which, because of their underlying assumptions, might elicit answers that falsified the experience. I approached the descriptions and explanations given by the adepts, researchers, and theorists as fictions; and I supposed that, like all fictions, they revealed truths about what someone who had the sensation of leaving his body went through.

But, although I had to be wary when dealing with the experience itself, there were certain questions about how people reacted to the idea of the experience—whether or not the phenomenon was real—which could not be ducked, questions which I had tried to deal with at various stages of my inquiry and which continued to haunt me because their significance went far beyond the limits of psychical research. A book on parapsychology may seem a strange stage for political speculation, but there appears to be a connection between politics and belief in the paranormal.

The frustrations which make one susceptible to out-of-the-body experiences also make one susceptible to the dangerous aspects of the theories based on those experiences. When people feel powerless in everyday reality, they seek power in other realities. If God can't save them since He no longer exists, then they turn to new gods—extraterrestrials who land spaceships on earth in time to avert some worldwide disaster (a plot common to 1950s science fiction movies and to 1970s out-of-the-body theorists) or superhumans who can sort out the confusion we cannot escape.

This demand for an explanation of the unknown feeds a fascination with the occult and the paranormal and sparks mass interest in psychic superstars like Uri Geller, who had spent the year I was researching this book strutting through the celebrity circuit. He had visited England two weeks before I had arrived to meet Robert Crookall; and, in his stage performances (which emphasized the *chic* in psychic), he gave demonstrations of telepathy and psychokinesis. His act was so convincing that he even persuaded a senior official at the American Embassy in London, who previously had been an unreconstructed skeptic.

In *Time Out*, a weekly entertainment magazine for London, a full-page advertisement for the Village Bookstore on Regent Street betrayed the anarchic connection between the occult and slapstick by joining Madame Blavatsky, the nineteenth-century founder of the Theosophical Society, with Groucho Marx in an imaginary conversation. Uri Geller bending keys through telekinesis (illusion or not) is the psychic equivalent of Groucho destroying language: both, like mad bombers on our airplane flight, force us to re-examine our well-organized realities.

"Don't you think he *can* bend those spoons with his

mind?" the American Embassy official had asked me. "I *saw* him do it."

"I *saw* him do it!" Behind the faddism stirred an uneasiness: If you can't trust your own eyes, then how can you be sure that the housebroken reality we are used to is, in fact, real?

After an iconoclastic century and a half, during which theories, doctrines, and dogmas in all fields staggered up and collapsed like clowns on a waxed floor, reality has become a shifty concept. In a world of quarks and positrons, quasars and black holes, our unamplified senses seem puny, inefficient, perhaps obsolete instruments for recording what is happening *out there* in external reality. Everything has become occult— which, after all, simply means hidden; and investigations into the paranormal are attempts to uncover the hidden. They are rational stabs at the irrational.

"We're in the same position Copernicus was in," one New York occultist told me while he tried to explain how he was one of the few true children of the Age of Reason. "We've got to rearrange society's conception of the universe and make it more realistic," by including astrology, palmistry, phrenology, dowsing, and alchemy in the liberal arts curriculum. If science can become a cult (on the M.I.T. campus and at the Houston Space Center), why can't cults become science— alchemists inspecting their alembics and retorts with the same professional intensity that NASA officials conjure a well-defined photograph out of the chaos of electrical impulses being transmitted from an interplanetary rocket back to earth.

The New York occultist was correct in thinking that our society's conception of the universe had to be revised—if only to bring it into phase with the proliferation of extraordinary discoveries made in the past century. We *are* suffering from future shock, and we will suffer until our assumptions about reality come into coincidence with our knowledge of reality. But this integration cannot occur until we develop a language which can mediate among the warring views of what the world is all about. God is no longer the common denominator to which all disciplines can be reduced. We no longer study the stars or ourselves for the glory of the Almighty. Our politics do not derive from a faith in an order grounded in the Eternal. Science cannot talk to politics; politics cannot talk to art. As a result, people, isolated within their idiosyncratic and merely functional beliefs, have no commerce—and therefore limited effect—beyond their immediate environment. They become functionless except as superintendents of their own fortunes. They are severed from any connections to a greater—either secular or sacred—good.

People need to feel a sense of personal worth; when a society suffers a crisis of confidence, like the one America is undergoing in the last third of the twentieth century, and when traditional value systems fail, people seize on any philosophy which can make them feel special. And that sense of being special can be translated into an elitism which I found manifest in many of the beliefs that had been developed from out-of-the-body experiences.

"Someone who's had an out-of-the-body experience is in a better position to make decisions concerning the fate of society than someone who hasn't," said one out-of-the-body researcher and adept. "He has more perspective."

"A person who has had these experiences is as superior to someone who hasn't as a man is to, say, his pet dog," said another. "And you wouldn't consult with your dog about how to run your household, would you?"

The frustrated seek increasing power, waiting for the sign that more power has graced them; and, having been plunged into an out-of-the-body experience, they may easily confuse an extraordinary reality with an extraordinary illusion. The egalitarian myth in which the pauper grows up to discover he is a prince and which is renewed in the comics when Clark Kent sneaks into a broom closet and reappears as Superman can be easily transformed into a totalitarian fable.

The conceit that paranormal abilities—if they exist—represent either mental, moral, or evolutionary superiority can be exploited to fashion the kind of supremacist politics that in the twentieth century has tended to feed off social and economic crises. My search through the psychic underworld repeatedly led me to this disturbing possibility. If the descriptions and explanations of the out-of-the-body experience are fictions, they are, like Grimms' fairy tales, stories in which the fantastic often flowers out of a loathsome root.

But, like kids listening to bedtime stories, eventually we ask of any fiction: Is it true? Because so many people who'd had the experience stressed how real it seemed, during my year of research I tried various methods for inducing an out-of-the-body episode, assuming that I might be less skeptical if I also had slipped from my skin.

For two weeks after I'd visited Robert Monroe, I experimented unsuccessfully with his deep-breathing techniques every morning upon waking. The day after I'd decided to scrap the experiment, I was lying in bed, listening to my wife running water in the bathroom sink, when I felt as though I were floating up into the air and slowly turning over. When I was about a foot and a half above the bed I was facing the mattress, looking at my body which was stretched out on its right side, eyes opened.

I thought, *This is obviously a dream, since I'm lying on my right side and Monroe said you have to lie on your back.*

I floated down, slowly turning around the opposite way, and re-entered my body. I closed and opened my eyes, listened to the sink-water running, assured myself that I was awake, and floated up out of my body again. It was difficult to concentrate on reality-testing. My mind wandered the way it does when I'm trying to go over a problem as I'm falling asleep. I kept drifting away from and then jerking back to the realization that I was having what seemed to be an out-of-the-body experience. My wife turned off the water in the bathroom; and, as though time had been folded like an accordion and two moments fifteen minutes apart adjoined, she was touching my shoulder, saying, "It's seven o'clock; are you getting up?"

I surfaced from a confused dream which dealt with trying to decide whether or not my out-of-the-body experience had been real; and although I assume that the experience itself had been part of that dream, I cannot be sure. When it happened, it had seemed real and I'd been convinced that I was awake.

I did wonder, however, how much a part my own recent exposure to the subject played in my out-of-the-body experience. As with many of the adepts I'd been studying, my sensation of consciousness separating from the flesh could have been induced—or at least encouraged—by a mind set that accepted the experience as possible.

The allure of the out-of-the-body phenomenon lies in the fact that the experience hints at a way of escaping, not only from the cage of scientific rationalism, but also from the frustrating box of the five senses. By promising direct perception of what is *out there*, the experience titillates the desire for an unblocked access to objective reality; it kindles our Faustian desire to *know*. But paranormal inquiry cannot, in the end, satisfy the appetite it encourages. Science can never replace revelation.

There is no doubt that the experience of separating from the body has a subjective reality. People do have the sensation of consciousness leaving the flesh and organizing itself from a point in space. And there is some evidence that an apparently disembodied consciousness can correctly perceive information at a distance. But the evidence, fragmentary and subject to differing interpretations, does not constitute proof that the experience has an objective reality. It is only an argument for further research.

I suspect, however, that further research will not be able to prove that the phenomenon is objectively real. The experience, from all the descriptions, seems to be, not an event, but a process, an interaction between what we experience as subjective and objective realities; and if the phenomenon exists outside of personal fantasies, it exists in that interface between those two realities.

In discussing the reality of the out-of-the-body experience, I still must say *if.* I have not been able to decide whether or not the experience is more than an intriguing fantasy. Because there is no proof, belief becomes an act of faith, a religious conversion.

Since every interpretation of the out-of-the-body phenomenon reflects the researcher's bias, I knew when starting this study that the investigation would become in part a search for self, an inquiry into how I would interpret the phenomenon. After a year's research, I am convinced only of the essential ambiguity of the experience. And I am left confronting a self which—suspended like a pin between two equally powerful magnetic fields—struggles alternately to believe and to disbelieve, unable to do either.

Bibliography

Ackerman, Albert. "Miracle Gurus of India," *Psychic*, Vol. 5, No. 2, November/December, 1973.

Allport, G.W. "The Eidetic Image and the After-Image," *American Journal of Psychology*, July, 1928.

Anesaki, Masaharu. *The Mythology of All Races: Japanese*, Vol. VIII, ed. Canon John Arnott MacCulloch. New York: Cooper Square Publishers, Inc., 1964.

Anon. "Astral Projection or How to Leave Your Body," unpublished. From Stanley Krippner, Dream Laboratory, Maimonides Medical Center.

Ashby, Robert H. "Some English Views on Survival," *Psychic*, Vol. 2, No. 5, March/April, 1971.

ASPR *Newsletter*. "ASPR Continues OOBE Talent Search," No. 20, Winter, 1974.

———— "ASPR Research Follows the Terms of the Kidd Will," No. 17, Spring, 1973.

———— "ASPR Symposium," No. 21, Spring, 1974.

———— "Reception for Ingo Swann," No. 14, Summer, 1972.

Bardens, Dennis. *Mysterious Worlds.* New York: Cowles Book Co., Inc., 1970.

Barrett, W.F. *Death-Bed Visions.* London: Methune, 1926.

Basham, A.L. *The Wonder That Was India.* New York: Grove Press, Inc., 1959.

Bateson, Gregory. *Steps To An Ecology Of Mind.* New York: Ballantine Books, 1972.

Beren, Peter Lee. "LSD Era: It All Started With a Mayonnaise Jar," *Boston Phoenix,* Dec. 25, 1973.

Berendt, H.C. "Parapsychology in Israel," *Parapsychology Review,* Vol. 3, No. 4, July/August, 1972.

Binet, Alfred. *On Double Consciousness.* Chicago: The Open Court Publishing Co., 1896.

Blunsdon, Norman. *A Popular Dictionary of Spiritualism.* New York: The Citadel Press, 1963.

Bohannan, Walter. "The Metabiology of the Unknown," *Scottish International Review,* Ltd., n.d.

Bolen, James Grayson. "Interview: Harold Sherman," *Psychic,* Vol. 5, No. 3, January/February, 1974.

———— "Interview: Rex G. Stanford," *Psychic,* Vol. 5, No. 5, May/June, 1974.

Booth, Albert B. *Science,* letter, Vol. 180, June 8, 1973.

Brennan, J.H. *Astral Doorways.* New York: Samuel Weiser, Inc., 1971.

Broad, C.D. *Lectures on Psychical Research Incorporating the Perott Lectures Given in Cambridge University in 1959 and 1960.* London: Routledge & Kegan Paul, 1962.

Buckley, Ken. "Looking Into The Future: ESP Artist Has Good Average," *Bangor Daily News,* Nov. 24, 1969.

Burbank, Russell P. "Tom Tanous: MTA President for 1974–75," *The Massachusetts Teacher,* May/June, 1974.

Burr, Harold Saxton. *The Fields of Life.* New York: Ballantine Books, 1973.

Burton, Larry, and Gaines, William. "Some Aspects of Kirlian Photography," paper presented at the Parapsychological Association Convention, University of Va., September, 1973.

Butler, Alban. *Butler's Lives of the Saints.* Edited, Revised, and Supplemented by Herbert Thurston, S.J. and Donald Attwater. New York: P.J. Kennedy & Sons, 1956.

Butler, Robert N. "The Life Review," *Psychology Today,* Vol. 5, No. 7, December, 1971.

Campbell, John Gregorson. *Witchcraft and Second Sight in the Highlands and Islands of Scotland: Tales and Traditions Collected Entirely from Oral Sources.* Detroit: Singing Tree Press, 1970. Facsimile reprint of the 1902 edition published by James MacLehoge and Sons, Glasgow.

Campbell, Joseph. *The Masks of God: Creative Mythology.* New York: The Viking Press, 1970.

———— *The Masks of God: Occidental Mythology.* New York: The Viking Press, 1970.

———— *The Masks of God: Oriental Mythology.* New York: The Viking Press, 1970.

———— *The Masks of God: Primitive Mythology.* New York: The Viking Press, 1970.

Caramadre, T.J. "Maine Psychic Entertains 1,600 with His Predictions." *The Observer-Dispatch,* Aug. 27, 1971.

Castaneda, Carlos. *Journey to Ixtlan.* New York: Ballantine Books, 1972.

———— *A Separate Reality.* New York: Ballantine Books, 1971.

———— *The Teachings of Don Juan.* New York: Ballantine Books, 1968.

Cavander, Kenneth. "Voyage of the Psychenauts." *Harper's,* January, 1974.

Cayce, Edgar. *Auras: An Essay on the Meaning of Colors.* Virginia Beach, Va.: A.R.E. Press, 1973.

Chance, Paul. "Parapsychology Is an Idea Whose Time Has Come." *Psychology Today,* Vol. 7, No. 5, October, 1973.

Choron, Jacques. *Modern Man and Mortality.* New York: The Macmillan Co., 1964.

Christopher, Melbourne. *E.S.P., Seers and Psychics.* New York: Thomas Y. Crowell, 1970.

Cohen, Daniel. *Masters of the Occult.* New York: Dodd, Mead & Co., 1970.

Coleman, Stanley M. "August Strindberg: the Autobiographies." *Psychoanalytic Review.* Vol. 23, 1936.

———— "The Phantom Double: Its Psychological Significance." *British Journal of Medical Psychology,* Vol. 14, 1934.

Cowan, Thaddeus M. *Science,* letter, Vol. 180, June 8, 1973.

Crookall, Robert. "Astral Traveling: Review of *The Enigma of Out-of-Body Travel* by Susy Smith." *International Journal of Parapsychology,* Vol. VIII, No. 3, Summer, 1966.

_____ *The Interpretation of Cosmic and Mystical Experiences.* Cambridge and London: James Clarke & Co., 1965.

_____ *The Mechanisms of Astral Projection: Denouement after Seventy Years.* Moradabad, India: Darshana International, 1968.

_____ *The Next World—and the Next.* London: The Theosophical Publishing House, Ltd., 1966.

_____ *Out-of-the-Body Experiences: A Fourth Analysis.* New York: University Books, Inc., 1970.

_____ *The Study and Practice of Astral Projection.* Secaucus, N.J.: University Books, Inc., 1966.

_____ *The Techniques of Astral Projection.* Denington Estate, Wellingborough, Northamptonshire: The Aquarian Press, 1964.

Crow, W.B. *A History of Magic, Witchcraft and Occultism.* London: The Aquarian Press, 1968.

Dalton, Buell W. "Position Paper on 'Communicating Thanatology—The Message and Method.'" Unpublished paper.

De Merchant, E.B. "Dr. Tanous: Maine Soothsayer Unforgettable Man." *The Telegraph-Journal*, St. John, N.B., Jan. 1, 1971.

_____ "Maine Psychologist Says: Understanding of Mind Last Major Frontier." *The Telegraph-Journal*, St. John, N.B., March 27, 1972.

de Vesme, Caesar. *Experimental Spiritualism: Vol. 1 Primitive Man; Vol. II Peoples of Antiquity.* London: Rider and Co., 1931.

Dewhurst, K., and Todd, J. "The Double: Psychopathology and Physiology," *Journal of Nervous and Mental Diseases*, Vol. 122, No. 47, 1955.

Douglas, Mary. *Natural Symbols: Explorations in Cosmology.* New York: Vintage Books, 1970.

Downey, June E. "Literary Self-Projection." *Psychological Review*, Vol. 19, July, 1912.

Downing, Paul. "Alex Tanous: A Vision of Darkness." *Maine Sunday Telegram*, May 16, 1971.

_____ "What A Maine Psychic Finds Touring Europe: Ghosts in a Dungeon, Murder from a Balcony." *Maine Sunday Telegram*, Sept. 5, 1971.

DuNoüy, Lecomte. *Human Destiny.* New York: Signet Books, New American Library, 1949.

Eastman, Margaret. "Out-of-the-Body Experiences." *Proceedings of the Society for Psychical Research*, Vol. 53, Part 193, December, 1962.

Edwards, Frank. *Strange Fate*. New York: Paperback Library, 1965.

Eisenbud, Jule. *The World of Ted Serios*. New York: William Morrow and Co., Inc., 1967.

Eliade, Mircea. *Myths, Dreams and Mysteries*. New York: Harper Torchbooks, 1967.

———— *The Sacred and the Profane: The Nature of Religion*. New York: Harvest Books, Harcourt, Brace and World, Inc., 1959.

———— *Shamanism: Archaic Techniques of Ecstasy*. Princeton, N.J.: Bollingen Series LXXVI, Princeton University Press, 1964.

———— "Time and Eternity in Indian Thought," in *Man and Time: Papers from the Eranos Yearbooks*, ed. Joseph Campbell. Princeton, N.J.: Bollingen Series XXX, No. 3, Pantheon, 1957.

Eranos Yearbook. *The Mysteries. Papers From the Eranos Yearbooks*. ed. Joseph Campbell. Princeton, N.J.: Bollingen Series XXX, No. 2, Princeton University Press, 1955.

———— *Spiritual Discipline: Papers From the Eranos Yearbooks*. Ed. by Joseph Campbell. New York: Bollingen Series XXX, No. 4, Pantheon, 1960.

ERG Laboratory. Memo to Karlis Osis from B.P. Re: Session 1 with Al Tanous at ERG Laboratory, March 4, 1974.

———— "Out of Body Experiment March, 1974 at ERG." Transcript.

Evans-Wentz, W.Y. *The Tibetan Book of the Dead*. London: Oxford University Press, 1960.

Fate Magazine editors. *Strange Fate*. New York: Paperback Library, 1965.

Feifel, Herman and Jones, Robert B. "Perception of Death as Related to Nearness to Death." *Proceedings, 76th Annual Convention, American Parapsychological Association*, 1968.

Feola, Jose M. "Psychical Theories and New Experimental Approaches to Research." *Psychic*, Vol. 1, No. 3, October/November, 1969.

Ferguson, John C. *The Mythology of All Races: Chinese*, Vol. VIII, ed. Canon John Arnott MacCulloch. New York: Cooper Square Publishers, Inc., 1964.

Fodor, Nandor. *The Haunted Mind.* New York: Signet Mystic Books, New American Library, 1968.

Ford, Arthur, told to Ellison, Jerome. *The Life Beyond Death.* Berkley Medallion Books, Berkley Publishing Corporation, 1972.

Fox, Oliver. *Astral Projection.* New Hyde Park, N.Y.: University Books, 1962.

Fox, William Sherwood. *The Mythology of All Races: Greek and Roman,* Vol. 1, ed. Louis Herbert Gray. Boston: Marshall Jones Co., 1916.

Franklin, Wilbur. *Physics Today,* letter, August, 1973.

Frazer, Sir James George. *The Golden Bough: Adonis, Attis, Osiris.* New York: Macmillan, St. Martin's Press, 1966.

———— *The Golden Bough: Taboo and the Perils of the Soul.* New York: Macmillan, St. Martin's Press, 1966.

Freedland, Nat. *The Occult Explosion.* New York: Putnam, 1972.

Freud, Sigmund. *Studies in Parapsychology.* New York: Collier Books, 1963.

Garrett, Eileen J. *Beyond the Five Senses.* Philadelphia: J.B. Lippincott Company, 1957.

———— *Many Voices: The Autobiography of a Medium.* New York: Dell Publishing Co., Inc., 1968.

Garrett, Robert. "They Prospect for Soul Proof." *New York Post,* Dec. 6, 1972.

Gauld, Alan. *The Founders of Psychical Research.* New York: Schocken Books, 1968.

Godwin, John. *Occult America.* New York: Doubleday, 1972.

Goethe, Johann Wolfgang von. *The Autobiography,* trans. by John Oxenford. New York: Horizon Press, 1969.

———— *Collected Works.* ed. F.H. Hedge and L. Nea. Boston: Estes and Lauriat, 1883.

Goodall, Kenneth. "Through Death's Door." *Psychology Today,* Vol. 6, No. 5, October, 1972.

Green, Celia. *Out-of-the-Body Experiences.* New York: Ballantine Books, 1968.

Grossberger, Lewis. "4 Imported Mediums Have a Message for the Media." *New York Post,* March 13, 1974.

Guerard, Albert J. *Stories of the Double.* Philadelphia: J.B. Lippincott Co., 1967.

Guntrip, Harry. *Schizoid Phenomena, Object Relations, and the Self.* New York: International Universities Press, 1969.

Gurney, E., Myers, F.W.H., and Podmore, F. *Phantasms of the Living.* New York: E.P. Dutton and Co., 1918.

Gwynne, Peter. "Parapsychology—What the Questionnaire Revealed." *New Scientist,* Jan. 25, 1973.

Hackett, Thomas P., and Cassem, Ned H. "Patients Facing Sudden Cardiac Death." *Medical Care,* n.d.

Hammond, Sally. "An Aura of Good Feeling." *New York Post,* Feb. 14, 1973.

Hart, Hornell. "ESP Projection: Spontaneous Cases and the Experimental Method." *Journal of the ASPR.* Vol. 48, No. 4, October, 1954.

_____ "Scientific Survival Research." *International Journal of Parapsychology,* Vol. 9, March, 1967.

Hastings, James. *Encyclopedia of Religion and Ethics,* Vol. IV, New York: Scribner's, 1928.

Haynes, Renée. *The Hidden Springs: An Enquiry Into Extrasensory Perception.* Boston: Little, Brown and Company, 1972.

Healey, T. *Science,* letter, Vol. 182, Oct. 19, 1973.

Herbert, Frank. "Listening to the Left Hand." *Harper's,* December, 1973.

Herodotus. *The Histories,* Vols. 1–4. London: William Heineman, 1930.

Heywood, Rosalind. "Attitudes to Death in the Light of Dreams and Other 'Out-of-the-Body' Experience." From *Man's Concern with Death* by Arnold Toynbee. New York: McGraw-Hill Book Co., 1968.

_____ *The Infinite Hive.* London: Pan Books Ltd., 1964.

Hoffmann, J. "Phantom Limb Syndrome: A Critical Review of Literature," *Journal of Nervous and Mental Diseases,* March, 1954.

Holmberg, Uno. *The Mythology of All Races,* Finno-Ugric, Siberian, Vol. IV, ed. Canon John Arnott MacCulloch. New York: Cooper Square Publishers, Inc. 1964.

Honorton, Charles; Davidson, Richard; and Bindler, Paul. "Feedback-Augmented EEG Alpha, Shifts in Subjective State, and ESP Card-Guessing Performance." *Journal of the ASPR,* Vol. 65, No. 3, July, 1971.

Honorton, C., Drucker, S.A.; and Hermon, H.C. "Shifts in Subjective State and ESP Under Conditions of Partial Sensory Deprivation: A Preliminary Study." *Journal of the ASPR,* Vol. 67, No. 2, April, 1973.

Honorton, Charles. "Significant Factors in Hypnotically Induced Clairvoyant Dreams." *Journal of the ASPR*, Vol. 66, No. 1, January, 1972.

Hook, Sidney. *Dimensions of Mind.* London: Collier Books, Collier-Macmillan Ltd., 1961.

Hull, David. "A Populational Approach to Scientific Change." *Science*, Vol. 182, Dec. 14, 1972.

Hunt, Douglas. *Exploring the Occult.* London: Pan Books Ltd., 1964.

Hunter, R.C.A. "On the Experience of Nearly Dying." *American Journal of Psychiatry*, Vol. 124, No. 1, July, 1967.

Hurwood, Bernhardt J. *The Second Occult Review Reader.* New York: Aware Books, 1969.

Hutchinson, Horace G. *Dreams and Their Meanings.* London: Longmans, Green, and Co., 1901.

Huxley, Aldous. *The Doors of Perception and Heaven & Hell.* London: Chatto & Windus, 1960.

_____ *Time Must Have a Stop.* New York: Perennial Classic Books, Harper and Row, 1965.

Hyslop, James H. *Psychical Research and the Resurrection.* Boston: Small, Maynard and Co., 1908.

Inge, William Ralph. *The Philosophy of Plotinus*, Vols. 1 and 2. London: Longmans, Green and Co., 1948.

Isherwood, Christopher. *Ramakrishna and His Disciples.* New York: Simon and Schuster. n.d.

Jacobson, Nils O., M.D. "Reincarnation: Evidence for Survival." *Psychic*, Vol. 5, No. 2, November/December, 1973.

Jacques, Steve. "Psychic Energy: the New Language of Perception." *Probe*, February, 1974.

Jaffé, Aniela. *From the Life and Work of C.G. Jung.* New York: Harper Colophon Books, 1971.

James, William. "A Possible Case of Projection of the Double," *Journal of the ASPR*, Vol. 2, No. 4, April, 1909.

_____ *The Varieties of Religious Experience.* New York: Longmans, Green, and Co., 1902.

_____ *William James on Psychical Research.* New York: Viking Compass, 1969.

Janis, Joseph; Hartwell, John; Levin, Jerry; Morris, Robert. "A Description of the Physiological Variables Connected with an Out-of-Body Study." Unpublished paper.

Joachim, Leland. "A Planetary Citizen." *Probe*, February, 1974.

Johnson, Martha Lynne. "Evidence for an Afterlife? The Kaulback-Garrett Cross-Correspondence." *Psychic*. Vol. 3, No. 1, July/August, 1971.

Joire, Paul. *Psychical and Supernormal Phenomena*. New York: Frederick A. Stokes Co., 1918.

Jones, Stacy V. "Device Tests for Life and Death." *New York Times*, December 9, 1972.

Journal of the Society for Psychical Research. "General Meeting." June, 1884.

Jung, C.G. *Aion: Researches into the Phenomenology of the Self, Second Edition*. Princeton, N.J.: Bollingen Series XX, Princeton University Press, 1968.

———— *Four Archetypes*. Princeton, N.J.: Bollingen Series XX, Princeton University Press, 1970.

———— *Man and His Symbols*. New York: Dell Publishing Co., Inc., 1968.

———— *Memories, Dreams, and Reflections*. New York: Vintage, 1963.

———— *The Structure and Dynamics of the Psyche Including "Synchronicity: An Acausal Connecting Principal," Second Edition*. Princeton, N.J.: Bollingen Series XX, Princeton University Press, 1969.

———— *Symbols of Transformation, Second Edition*. Princeton, N.J.: Bollingen Series XX, Princeton University Press, 1967.

Kahn, Richard D. "Kidd Estate Funds Received." ASPR Newsletter, No. 17, Spring, 1973.

Kastenbaum, Robert, and Aisenberg, Ruth. *The Psychology of Death*. New York, Springer Publishing Co., Inc., 1972.

Keen, Sam. "From Dolphins to LSD—A Conversation with John Lilly." *Psychology Today*, Vol. 5, No. 7, December, 1971.

Keppler, C.F. *The Literature of the Second Self*. Tucson, Arizona: The University of Arizona Press, 1972.

Kerney, Chaplain LeRoy G. "Pastoral Use of 'The Seven Last Words' in Terminal Care." *Ethical Issues*, n.d.

Kilner, Walter J. *The Human Atmosphere*. New York: Rebman Company, 1911.

King, Frances. *Astral Projection: Magic and Alchemy*. New York: Samuel Weiser, Inc., 1972.

Kirlian, Semyon D., and Kirlian, Valentina. "Photography by Means of High-Frequency Currents." From *The Kirlian Aura*, ed. Stanley Krippner and Daniel Rubin. New York: Anchor, 1974.

Kitagawa, Joseph M., and Long, Charles H. *Myths and Symbols: Studies in Honor of Mircea Eliade*. Chicago: University of Chicago Press, 1969.

Koestler, Arthur. *The Roots of Coincidence*. New York: Vintage Books, 1973.

Krippner, Stanley, and Easton, Harry. "The Existential Theme in Jungian Psychology." *Journal of Contemporary Psychotherapy*, Vol. 3, No. 1, Summer, 1970.

Krippner, Stanley, and Rubin, Daniel. *The Kirlian Aura: Photographing the Galaxies of Life*. Garden City, N.Y.: Anchor Books, 1974.

Krippner, Stanley, and Zirinsky, Kenneth. "An Experiment in Dreams, Clairvoyance, and Telepathy." *The Association for Research and Enlightenment Journal*, Vol. 6, January, 1971.

Krippner, Stanley. "Experimentally Induced Effects in Dreams and Other Altered Conscious States." Paper prepared for 20th International Congress of Psychology, August 13–19, 1972, Tokyo, Japan.

———— "The Implications of Contemporary Dream Research." *Journal of the American Society of Psychosomatic Dentistry and Medicine*, Vol. 18, No. 3.

Landau, L. "An Unusual Out-of-Body Experience," *Journal of the Society for Psychical Research*, Vol. 42, Sept., 1963.

Leadbeater, C.W. *The Inner Life*. Madras, India: Theosophical Press, 1914.

———— *Invisible Helpers*. London: Theosophical Press, 1915.

Leake, Chauncey. *Science*, letter, Vol. 180, June 8, 1973.

LeShan, Lawrence. *The Medium, the Mystic, and the Physicist: Toward a General Theory of the Paranormal*. New York: The Viking Press, 1974.

Lethbridge, T.C. *Ghost and Ghoul*. New York: Doubleday, 1962.

Lewis, I.M. *Ecstatic Religion: An Anthropological Study of Spirit Possession and Shamanism*. Middlesex, England: Penguin Books, 1971.

Lhermitte, Jean. "Visual Hallucinations of the Self." *British Medical Journal*, March 3, 1951.

Liljeholm, Lyn. "Thornton Academy Proves ESP Works; In an Elective, Anyway." *Portland Sunday Telegram*, Dec. 24, 1972.

Lilly, John C. *The Center of the Cyclone: An Autobiography of Inner Space.* New York: The Julian Press, 1972.

_____ "Inner Space and Parapsychology." *Proceedings—Parapsychological Association,* No. 6, 1969.

_____ *Programming and Metaprogramming in the Human Biocomputer.* New York: Julian Press, 1972.

Lippman, Caro W. "Hallucinations of Physical Duality in Migraine." *Journal of Nervous and Mental Diseases,* Vol. 117, 1953.

London, Jack. *The Star Rover.* London: The Macmillan Company, Collier Macmillan Ltd., 1963.

Lukianowicz, N. "Autoscopic Phenomena." *American Medical Association Archives of Neurology and Psychiatry,* Vol. 80, No. 2, August, 1958.

MacCulloch, John Arnott. *The Mythology of All Races:* Eddic, Vol. II, ed. Canon John Arnott MacCulloch. New York: Cooper Square Publishers, Inc., 1904.

_____ *The Mythology of All Races:* Celtic, Volume III, ed. Louis Herbert Gray. Boston: Marshall Jones Co., 1908.

MacDonald, Bill. "Singer Back From the Dead With Fear for the Unknown." *Midnight,* August 20, 1973.

MacDonald, Glenn. "Commentary." *Lincoln County News,* September 3, 1970.

Máchal, Jan. *The Mythology of All Races: Slavic,* Vol. III, ed. Louis Herbert Gray. Boston: Marshall Jones Co., 1908.

MacKenzie, Norman. *Dreams and Dreaming.* New York: Vanguard Press, 1965.

McConnell, R.A. "Parapsychology and the Occult." *Journal of the ASPR,* Vol. 67, No. 3, July, 1973.

_____ "Parapsychology: Its Future Organization and Support." *Journal of the ASPR,* Vol. 68, No. 2, April, 1974.

McCormick, Jane L. "Psychic Phenomena in Literature." *Psychic,* Vol. 3, No. 4, January/February, 1972.

McCreery, Charles. *Psychical Phenomena and the Physical World.* New York: Ballantine Books, 1973.

Maimonides Medical Center, Department of Psychiatry, William C. Menninger Dream Laboratory. "An Analysis of Dream Content, Part I: Rules for Determining Units of Meaning in Dream Protocols." Unpublished paper, February, 1967.

_____ "An Analysis of Dream Content, Part II: Directions for Scoring Units of Meaning on Content Checklists." Unpublished paper, February, 1968.

———— "Dream Studies and Telepathy Experimental Series V (The Hypnosis Study)". Unpublished paper, June, 1967.

———— "Dream Studies and Telepathy Experimental Series VII (The Second Erwin Study)." Unpublished paper, February, 1969.

———— "Dream Studies and Telepathy Experimental Series VIII (Preliminary Report)." Unpublished paper, July, 1969.

———— "Dream Studies and Telepathy Experimental Series XI (Preliminary Report) The First Bessent Study." Unpublished paper, July, 1970.

———— "Dream Studies and Telepathy Preliminary Report, Experimental Series III (The Replication Study)." Unpublished paper, June, 1966.

———— "Dream Studies and Telepathy: Preliminary Report of Findings Experimental Series VI (The Grayeb Study)." Unpublished paper, December, 1967.

———— "Dream Studies and Telepathy: Preliminary Report, Experimental Series X, The Vaughan Study." Unpublished paper, 1971.

———— "Experimental Series I: The Preliminary Study, Report of Findings." Unpublished paper, January, 1965.

———— "Experimental Series II: The First Erwin Study, Report of Findings." Unpublished paper, October, 1965.

———— "Experimental Series XII, the Second Bessent Study: Preliminary Report." Unpublished paper, June, 1971.

———— "Extrasensory Electroencephalographic Induction: Progress Report." Unpublished paper, February, 1969.

———— "Subject: Jim Ungar; Date: June 30, 1966; Agent: C. Ezell; Experimenters: Don Smoot, Tony Cillaffo, Stan Krippner." Tape transcript, July 11, 1966.

———— "Subject: Jim Ungar; Date: July 28, 1966; Agent: Stan Krippner: Experimenters: John Kauth, Don Smoot, Gordon Kinder." Tape transcript, Aug. 6, 1966.

———— "Subject: Jim Ungar; Date: Aug. 11, 1966; Agent: Gordon Kinder; Experimenters: John Kauth, Don Smoot." Tape transcript, Sept. 28, 1966.

———— "Subject: Jim Ungar; Date: Aug. 18, 1966; Agent: Don Smoot; Experimenters: Stan Krippner; John Kauth." Tape transcript, Oct. 5, 1966.

Mar, Alan. "Psychic Helps Police Solve a Murder Case." *National Enquirer,* March 4, 1973.

Markfield, Alan. "Family's 200-Year-Old House Is Haunted By Ghost of a Murderess." *National Enquirer*, May 26, 1972.

MD. "Themes for Dreams Transmitted to Sleepers." July, 1965.

Melzack, Ronald. "Phantom Limbs." *Psychology Today*, Vol. 4, No. 5, October, 1970.

Michelet, Jules. *Satanism and Witchcraft*. Secaucus, N.J.: Lyle Stuart, Inc., 1939.

Milburn, Lucy McDowell. *The Classic of Spiritism*. New York: The Dacrow Co., 1922.

Miller, R. DeWitt. *Stranger Than Life*. New York: Ace Books, 1955.

Miree, Gayle. "Investigations of 'Psychic' Phenomena in Dreams and other Altered States of Consciousness." Unpublished paper.

Mitchell, Edgar D. "An Adventure in Consciousness." *Psychic*, Vol. 4, No 2, November/December, 1972.

_____ "Death and Consciousness." *Journal of Altered States of Consciousness*, Vol. 1, No. 1, Fall, 1973.

_____ "The Institute of Noetic Studies." *Psychic*, Vol. 4, No. 6, July/August, 1973.

_____ "Noetics, The Emerging Science of Consciousness." *Psychic*, Vol. 4, No. 4. March/April, 1973.

Mitchell, Edgar D., and White, John. *Psychic Exploration*. New York: G.P. Putnam's Sons, 1974.

Mitchell, Janet. "Out-of-the-body Vision." *Psychic*, Vol. 4, No. 4, March/April, 1973.

Monroe, Robert A. *Journeys Out of the Body*. Garden City, N.Y.: Anchor Books, 1973.

Morris, Robert L. "Animals and ESP." *Psychic*, Vol. 5, No. 1, September/October, 1973.

_____ "Survival: Parapsychology's Toughest Question?" *Proceedings—Parapsychological Association*, No. 8, 1971.

_____ "Survival Research at the Psychical Research Foundation." *ASPR News*. No. 18, Summer, 1973.

_____ "A Two-Year Project of Survival Research: Six-Month Progress Report." Unpublished paper.

Morris, Robert L.; Janis, Joseph M.; and Levin, Jerry. "The Use of Detectors for Out-of-Body Experiences." Unpublished paper.

Morris, Robert L.; Hartwell, John; Janis, Joseph M.; and Levin, Jerry. "A Description of the Psychological Variables Connected with an Out-of-Body Study." Unpublished paper.

Moss, Thelma, and Johnson, Ken. "Radiation Field Photography." *Psychic*, Vol. 3, No. 6, July/August, 1972.

Muldoon, Sylvan. *The Case for Astral Projection*. Chicago: The Aries Press, 1936.

―――― *Hallucination or Reality: The Case for Astral Projection*. Chicago: The Aries Press, 1936.

Muldoon, Sylvan, and Carrington, Hereward. *The Phenomena of Astral Projection*. New York: Samuel Weiser, Inc., 1972.

―――― *The Projection of the Astral Body*. New York: Samuel Weiser, Inc., 1973.

Müller, F. Max, trans. *The Upanishads*. New York: Dover Publications, Inc., 1962.

Murphy, Gardner. *Challenge of Psychical Research: A Primer of Parapsychology*. New York: Harper Colophon Books, 1970.

―――― *Three Papers on the Survival Problem*. New York: The American Society for Psychical Research, Inc., n.d.

Myers, F. W. H. *Human Personality and Its Survival of Bodily Death*. London: Longmans, Green and Co., 1919.

Neubert, Robert W. "The Sects and Memberships of an Obscured Order." *Psychic*, Vol. 1, No. 6, May/June, 1970.

Neumann, Erich. *The Origins and History of Consciousness*. Princeton, N.J.: Bollingen Series XLII, Princeton University Press, 1954.

Newsweek. "ESP and the Dreamer." May 24, 1965.

New York Post. "Soulful Weight-Watcher." Dec. 19, 1972.

Noyes, Russell Jr. "The Art of Dying." *Perspectives in Biology and Medicine*, Spring, 1971.

―――― "Dying and Mystical Consciousness." *Journal of Thanatology*, Vol. 1, January/February, 1971.

―――― "The Experience of Dying." *Psychiatry*, Vol. 35, May, 1972.

Noyes, Russell Jr., and Kletti, Roy. "The Experience of Dying From Falls." *Omega*, Southern Illinois University School of Medicine, Vol. 3, 1972.

O'Regan, Brendan. "Perspective: Now You see it, now . . . ?" *New Scientist*, July 12, 1973.

Osis, Karlis. *Deathbed Observations by Physicians and Nurses*. New York: Parapsychology Foundation, Inc., 1961.

―――― "Deathbed Observations in India." *ASPR Newsletter*, No. 19, Autumn, 1973.

_____ "New ASPR Research on Out-of-the-Body-Experiences."
ASPR Newsletter, No. 14, Summer, 1972.

_____ "Perspectives for Out-of-Body Research." Unpublished
paper.

Ostrander, Sheila, and Schroeder, Lynn. *Psychic Discoveries Behind the Iron Curtain.* Englewood Cliffs, N.Y.: Prentice-Hall,
Inc., 1970.

Ouspensky, P.D. *The Fourth Way.* New York: Knopf, 1957.

_____ *In Search of the Miraculous.* New York: Harvest Books,
Harcourt, Brace and World, Inc., 1949.

Pahnke, Walter N. "The Psychedelic Mystical Experience in the
Human Encounter With Death." *Psychedelic Review*, No. 1,
Winter, 1970.

Palmer, John. "A Psychological Theory of Out-of-the-Body Experiences." Unpublished paper.

_____ "Research on Out-of-the-Body Experiences: Where Do
We Go From Here." Paper presented at the Parapsychology
Symposium, University of Virginia, September, 1973.

_____ "Scoring in ESP Tests as a Function of Belief in ESP, Part
I. The Sheep-Goat Effect." *Journal of the ASPR*, Vol. 65, No.
4, October, 1971.

_____ "Scoring in ESP Tests as a Function of Belief in ESP, Part
II. Beyond the Sheep-Goat Effect." *Journal of the ASPR*, Vol.
66, No. 1, January, 1972.

Palmer, John, and Lieberman, Ronald. "Proposed Abstract: Para-
psychological Association Convention, August, 1974: ESP and
Out-of-the-Body Experiences: The Effect of Psychological Set."
Unpublished paper.

Palmer, John, and Vassar, Carol. "Research Brief: Toward Experimental Induction of the Out-of-the-Body Experience." Paper
presented at the Convention of the American Parapsychology
Society, University of Virginia, September, 1973.

Pearce, Joseph Chilton. *The Crack in the Cosmic Egg.* New York:
Pocket Books, 1973.

Plessner, Helmuth. "On the Relationship of Time to Death," in *Man
and Time: Papers from the Eranos Yearbooks*, ed. Joseph
Campbell. Princeton, N.J.: Bollingen Series XXX, No. 3, Pantheon, 1957.

Pliny. *The Natural History of Pliny*, Vol. II. London: Henry G.
Bohn, 1855.

Plotinus. *Collected Works*, trans. by Stephen MacKenna. London: Faber and Faber. 1962.

Podmore, Frank. *Mediums of the Nineteenth Century*, Vol. 2. New Hyde Park, N.Y.: University Books, Inc., 1963.

Powell, A.E. *The Astral Body*. Wheaton, Ill.: The Theosophical Publishing House, 1973.

———— *The Etheric Double*. Wheaton, Ill.: The Theosophical Publishing House, 1969.

Poynton, J.C. "Parapsychology in South Africa." *Parapsychology Review*, Vol. 3, No. 2, March/April, 1972.

Prat, S., and Schlemmer, J. "Electrography." *Journal of the Biological Photographic Association*, 1939.

Pratt, J.G. "In Memory of Hornell Hart: A Personal Appreciation." *Journal of the ASPR*, Vol. 62, No. 1, January, 1968.

———— "Some Notes for the Future Einstein for Parapsychology." *Journal of the ASPR*, Vol. 68, No. 2, April, 1974.

Price, H.H. "What Kind of Next World." From *Man's Concern With Death* by Arnold Toynbee. New York: McGraw-Hill Book Co., 1968.

Prince, Walter Franklin. *They Saw Beyond*. New York: The Olympia Press, Inc., 1972.

Proclus. *The Elements of Theology*. Oxford: The Clarendon Press, 1963.

Progoff, Ira. *Jung's Psychology and Its Social Meaning*. Garden City, N.Y.: Anchor Books, 1973.

———— *The Symbolic and the Real*. New York: McGraw-Hill Book Company, 1973.

Psychic. "About the Cover." Vol. 3, No. 6; July/August, 1972.

———— "Interview: Andrija Puharich, M.D." Vol. 5, No. 1, September/October, 1973.

———— "Interview: Ingo Swann." Vol. 4, No. 4, March/April, 1973.

———— "Interview: Ray Stanford." Vol. 5, No. 4, March/April, 1974.

———— "A Special Report: Information from SRI." Vol. 4, No. 4, March/April, 1973.

Psychical Research Foundation, W.G. Roll, Project Director. "Summary: A Proposal to Explore Transpersonal Consciousness." Unpublished paper.

Puharich, Andrija. *Beyond Telepathy*. Garden City, N.Y.: Anchor Books, 1973.

_____ *A Journal of the Mystery of Uri Geller.* Garden City, N.Y.:
Anchor Press, 1974.

_____ *The Sacred Mushroom: Key to the Door of Eternity.* Garden City, N.Y.: Doubleday and Company, Inc., 1959.

_____ "Uri Geller and Extraterrestrials." *Psychic,* Vol. 5, No. 5, May/June, 1974.

Rachleff, Owen S. *The Occult Conceit.* Chicago: Cowles Book Co., Inc., 1971.

Rank, Otto. *The Double: A Psychoanalytic Study.* Chapel Hill: The University of North Carolina Press, 1971.

Rave, C.G. *Psychology As a Natural Science Applied to the Solution of Occult Psychic Phenomena.* Philadelphia: Porter and Coates, 1889.

Rawcliffe, D.H. *Illusions and Delusions of the Supernatural and the Occult.* New York: Dover Publications, Inc., 1959.

Reich, Wilhelm. *Ether, God and Devil: Cosmic Superimposition.* New York: Farrar, Straus and Giroux, 1973.

Richet, Charles. *Thirty Years of Psychical Research,* trans. by Stanley DeBrath. New York: Macmillan Co., 1923.

Rigali, Romola. "She Calls Herself a 'Sensitive.' " *Springfield Republican,* April 28, 1974.

Roberts, Jane. *The Seth Materials.* Englewood Cliffs, N.J.: Prentice-Hall, Inc., 1970.

Rogers, Robert. *A Psychoanalytic Study of the Double in Literature.* Detroit: Wayne State University Press, 1970.

Rogo, D. Scott. "Astral Projection in Tibetan Buddhist Literature." *International Journal of Parapsychology,* Vol. 10, No. 3, August, 1968.

_____ "Fakers and Fakirs." *Psychic,* Vol. 5, No. 2, November/December, 1973.

_____ "Out-of-the-Body Experiences." *Psychic,* Vol. 4, No. 4, March/April, 1973.

Róheim, Géza. *The Gates of the Dream.* New York: International Universities Press, Inc., 1952.

Roll, W.G. "A Proposal To Explore Transpersonal Consciousness," Unpublished paper.

_____ "Opinion: Might Consciousness Itself Be the Ultimate Tool in Parapsychology?" *Psychic,* Vol. 5, No. 3, January/February, 1974.

Rosenfeld, C. "The Shadow Within," *Daedalus,* Spring, 1967.

Rosicrucian Order. *Mastery of Life.* n.d.

Rumford Falls Times. "E.S.P. Lecturer in Rumford." March 30, 1972.

Russell, Bertrand. *A History of Western Philosophy.* New York: Simon and Schuster, 1945.

Ryzl, Milan. *Parapsychology: A Scientific Approach.* New York: Hawthorne Books, Inc., 1970.

Sarles, Harvey B. *Science.* letter, Vol. 180, June 8, 1973.

Scarf, Maggie. "Oh, for a Decent Night's Sleep!" *The New York Times Magazine,* October 21, 1973.

Schmeidler, Gertrude. "The Psychic Personality." *Psychic,* Vol. 5, No. 4, March/April, 1974.

———— "PK Effects Upon Continuously Recorded Temperature," *Journal of the ASPR,* Vol. 67, No. 4, October, 1973.

Schreiber, Flora Rheta and Herman, Melvin. "What Psychiatry Is Doing About E.S.P." *Science Digest,* February, 1966.

Science Digest. "Receivers' Dreams Are Related to Senders' View of Pictures." October, 1966.

Science News. "Physiology of the Phantom Limb." Vol. 105, No. 19, May 11, 1974.

Scientific American. Altered States of Awareness: Readings from Scientific American. San Francisco: W.A. Freeman and Co., 1972.

Seafield, Frank. *The Literature and Curiosities of Dreams,* Vols. I and II. London: Chapman and Hall, 1865.

Seligmann, Kurt. *Magic, Supernaturalism and Religion.* New York: Pantheon Books, 1948.

Shallice, Tim. "Mental States and Processes." *Science,* Vol. 183, March 15, 1974.

Shirley, Ralph. *The Mystery of the Human Double.* New Hyde Park, N.Y.: University Books, 1965.

Smith, Susy. *The Enigma of Out-of-Body Travel.* New York: Helix Press, Garrett Publications, 1965.

———— *E.S.P.* New York: Pyramid Publications, Inc., 1962.

———— *Out-of-Body Experiences for the Millions.* New York: Dell Books, Dell Publishing Co., Inc., 1969.

———— *Susy Smith's Supernatural World.* New York: Macfadden-Bartell Books, 1971.

Spraggett, Allen. *The Unexplained.* New York: Signet Mystic Books, New American Library, 1967.

Sprigge, Elizabeth. *The Strange Life of August Strindberg.* New York: The Macmillan Co., 1949.

Springfield Union. "Dying Taboo: Death As a Fact of Life." Nov. 23, 1972.

Stapledon, Olaf. *The Starmaker.* New York: Berkley Medallion Books, 1961.

Steegmuller, Francis. *Maupassant: A Limla The Path.* New York: Random House, 1949.

Steiger, Brad. *Mind Through Space and Time.* New York: Award Books, 1971.

———— *The Psychic Feats of Olaf Jonsson.* Englewood Cliffs, N.J.: Prentice-Hall, Inc., 1971.

Stevenson, Ian. "Some Psychological Problems Relevant to Research in Survival." *Theta,* No. 7, Fall, 1964.

Stone, Irving. *Jack London, Sailor on Horseback.* New York: Pocket Books, Inc., 1961.

Stratton, F.J.M. "An Account by Dr. X of "An Out-of-the-Body Experience Combined with ESP," *Journal of the Society for Psychical Research,* June, 1957.

Strindberg, August. *The Inferno.* London: William Rider and Son, Ltd., 1912.

Summers, Montague. *The History of Witchcraft.* Secaucus, N.J.: Lyle Stuart, Inc., 1956.

Swann, Ingo. "Out-of-Body Experiences." *ASPR Newsletter,* No. 14, Summer, 1972.

Tabori, Paul. *Pioneers of the Unknown.* New York: Taplinger Publishing Co., 1972.

Tart, Charles T. *Altered States of Consciousness.* Garden City, N.Y.: Anchor Books, 1969.

———— "A Psychophysiological Study of OOBE in a Selected Subject," *Journal of the ASPR,* Vol. 62, No. 1, January, 1968.

———— "Applications of Instrumentation in the Investigation of Haunting and Poltergeist Cases." *Journal of the ASPR,* Vol. 59, No. 3, July, 1965.

———— "A Second Study of OOBE," *The International Journal of Parapsychology,* December, 1967.

———— "Concerning the Scientific Study of the Human Aura." *Journal of the Society for Psychical Research.* Vol. 46, No. 751, March, 1972.

_____ "ESPATESTER: An Automatic Testing Device for Para-psychological Research." *Journal of the ASPR*, Vol. 60, No. 3, July, 1966.

_____ "A Further Psychophysiological Study of Out-of-the-Body Experiences in a Gifted Subject." *Proceedings—Parapsychological Association*, No. 6, 1969.

_____ "Hypnosis, Psychedelics, and Psi: Conceptual Models." In R. Cavanna and M. Ullman (eds.) *Psi and Altered States of Consciousness.* New York: Garrett Press, 1968.

_____ "Models for the Explanation of Extrasensory Perception." *International Journal of Neuropsychiatry*, Vol. 2, No. 5, 1966.

_____ "Out-of-the-Body Experiences by Celia Green Reviewed." *Theta*, Vol. 25, 1969.

_____ "A Possible 'Psychic' Dream, With Some General Speculations on the Nature of Such Dreams." *Journal of the Society for Psychical Research*, Vol. 42, No. 720, 1963.

_____ "A Psychophysiological Study of Out-of-the-Body Experiences in a Selected Subject." *The Journal of the ASPR*, Vol. 62, No. 1, January, 1968.

_____ "Physiological Correlates of Psi Cognition." *International Journal of Parapsychology*, Vol. 5, No. 4, Autumn, 1963.

_____ *Science*, letter, Vol. 180, June 8, 1973.

_____ "A Second Psychophysiological Study of Out-of-the-Body Experiences in a Gifted Subject." *International Journal of Parapsychology*, Vol. 9, December, 1967.

_____ "States of Consciousness and State-Specific Sciences." *Science*, Vol. 176, June 16, 1972.

_____ "Towards the Experimental Control of Dreaming: A Review of the Literature." *Psychological Bulletin*, Vol. 64, No. 1, August, 1965.

Tart, Charles T., and Smith, Jeffrey. "Two Token Object Studies with Peter Hurkos." *Journal of the ASPR*, Vol. 62, No. 2, April, 1968.

Tertullian. *Apologetic and Practical Treatises.* Oxford: John Henry Parker, 1854.

Theta. No. 29, Fall, 1970.

_____ No. 30, Winter, 1971.

_____ "Symposium on 'What Next in Survival Research?' " No. 5, Spring, 1964.

Thibodeau, Clement D. "Is It Proper to Print Dr. Tanous' Predictions in Church World?" *The Church World*, Jan. 24, 1969.

Thompson, Gordon T. "Federal Grant Supports ESP Dream Research at Maimonides." *New York Times*, Nov. 25, 1973.

Tickell, Mrs. J., "An Account of Experiences of Racing Motorists," *Journal of the Society for Psychical Research*, Vol. XLI, No. 62.

Tietze, Thomas R. "The Great Physical Mediums, Part 1." *Psychic*, Vol. 5, No. 2, November/December, 1973.

———"The Great Physical Mediums, Part 2." *Psychic*, Vol. 5, No. 3, January/February, 1974.

——— "Some Perspectives on Survival." *Psychic*, Vol. 3, No. 1, July/August, 1971.

Time. "The Pleasures of Dying." Dec. 4, 1972.

Tobias, Andrew. "Okay, He Averted World War III, But Can He Bend a Nail?" *New York*, September 10, 1973.

Tompkins, Peter and Bird, Christopher. *The Secret Life of Plants.* New York: Harper and Row, 1973.

Toth, Robert C. "White House Image? Just Ghostly." *Boston Globe*, July 9, 1973.

Toynbee, Arnold (and others). *Man's Concern with Death.* New York: McGraw-Hill, 1968.

Trotter, Robert J. "Transcendental Meditation." *Science News*, Vol. 104, Dec. 15, 1973.

Tyrrell, G.N.M. *Apparitions.* New York: Collier Books, 1963.

Ullman, Montague and Krippner, Stanley. "Dream Telepathy." *ASPR Newsletter*, No. 18, Summer, 1973.

Underhill, Evelyn. *Mysticism.* New York: E.P. Dutton and Co., Inc., 1961.

Van de Castle, Robert. "Anthropology and ESP." *Psychic*, Vol. 5, No. 3, January/February, 1974.

Vaughan, Alan. "Does Man Survive Death." *Psychic*, Vol. 2, No. 6, July/August, 1971.

——— "A Dream Grows in Brooklyn." *Psychic*, Vol. 1, No. 4, January/February, 1970.

——— "Interview: Rosalind Heywood." *Psychic*, Vol. 5, No. 2, November/December, 1973.

——— "The Media and Parapsychology." *Psychic*, Vol. 5, No. 5, May/June, 1974.

Wade, Nicholas. "Psychical Research: The Incredible in Search of Credibility." *Science*, Vol. 131, July 13, 1973.

Walkenstein, Eileen, M.D. "The Death Experience in Insulin Coma Treatment." *American Journal of Psychiatry*, Vol. 112, June, 1956.

Walker, Kenneth. *A Study of Gurdjieff's Teaching.* London: Jonathan Cape, 1965.

Watson, Lyall. *Supernature.* Garden City, N.Y.: Doubleday-Anchor, 1973.

Watts, Alan. *Nature, Man, and Woman.* New York: Vintage Books, 1958.

Webb, James. *The Flight From Reason* (Vol. I of The Age of the Irrational). London: MacDonald and Co., Inc., 1971.

Weed, Joseph S. *Wisdom of the Mystic Master.* West Nyack, N.Y.: Parker Publishing Co., Inc., 1968.

Weil, Andrew T. "The Natural Mind—A New Way of Looking at the Higher Consciousness." *Psychology Today,* Vol. 6, No. 5, October, 1972.

West, Louis Jolyon. *Hallucinations.* New York: Grune and Stratton, 1962.

White, John. *The Highest State of Consciousness.* Garden City, N.Y.: Anchor Books, 1972.

Whiteman, J.H.M. "The Process of Separation and Return in Experiences Fully 'Out of the Body.' " *Proceedings of the Society for Psychical Research,* Vol. 50, Part 185, May, 1956.

Whittaker, Thomas. *The Neo-Platonists: A Study in the History of Hellenism.* Cambridge: The University Press, 1901.

Wilson, Colin. *The Occult.* New York: Vintage Books, 1973.

Wise, Carroll A. "Response to the Threat of Death, Immediate and/or Postponed." Unpublished paper, 1972–1973.

Wolfe, Bernard. "Will Dolphins Rule the Universe?" *Oui,* May, 1973.

Wyndham, Horace. *Mr. Sludge, The Medium.* London: Geoffrey Bles, 1937.

Yates, Frances A. *Giordano Bruno and the Hermetic Tradition.* New York: Vintage Books, 1969.

Yogananda, Paramahansa. *Autobiography of a Yogi.* Los Angeles, Cal.: Self-Realization Fellowship, 1972.

Yram. *Practical Astral Projection.* New York: Samuel Weiser, Inc., 1972.

Zimmer, Heinrich. "Death and Rebirth in the Light of India," in *Man and Transformation: Papers from the Eranos Yearbooks,* ed. Joseph Campbell. Princeton, New Jersey: Bollingen Series XXX, No. 5, Pantheon, 1964.

INDEX

237